READING & ANALYZING
nonfiction

SLANT, SPIN & BIAS

Prestwick House

Writer
Douglas Grudzina

Senior Editor
Paul Moliken

Cover and Text Design
Maria J. Mendoza

Production
Jeremy Clark

Prestwick House

© 2009 Copyright Prestwick House, Inc.

ISBN: 978-1-60389-118-9

TABLE of Contents

5   **Introduction:** How to Use This Book

8   **Acknowledgments**

11   **Chapter One:** What is Nonfiction?

13   **Chapter Two:** The Elements of Nonfiction

      Fact 13

          Analysis of Fact 13

          Interpretation 16

          Exercise One 17

      Opinion 18

          Exercise Two 19

          Exercise Three 21

25   **Chapter Three:** Slant, Spin, and Bias

      "Half-Baked Alaska," by Toby Barlow 27

      "Officer Assaulted While Investigating Home Invasion" 35

      "Homecoming Marred by Police Harassment" 37

          Exercise One 39

      "The Unanimous Declaration of the Thirteen United States of America"...43

      "Why Women Should Vote," by Arthur Brisbane 50

          Exercise Two 53

      "When Will Woman's Mental Life Begin?" by Arthur Brisbane 56

          Exercise Three 61

          Writing Opportunity One 63

65   **Chapter Four:** Informative and Entertaining Nonfiction

      "Grant and Lee: A Study in Contrasts," by Bruce Catton 66

          Exercise One 72

      "Destination America: Mount Rushmore," by Tony Perrottet 76

          Exercise Two 88

      "Declaration of Sentiments and Resolutions," by Elizabeth Cady Stanton and Lucretia Mott 92

          Exercise Three 99

103 **Chapter Five:** Persuasive Nonfiction

      "All the Lonely People," by Rick Attig and Doug Bates 105

          Exercise One 110

"One Flew Out of the Cuckoo's Nest," by Rick Attig and Doug Bates ...112

    Exercise Two 116

"A Mad and Mindless Health Policy," by Rick Attig and Doug Bates.....119

    Writing Opportunity One 124

"On Women's Right to Vote," by Susan B. Anthony.............................125

    Exercise Three...128

"Battle of the Babies," by Agnes Repplier...130

    Exercise Four 138

    Writing Opportunity Two..139

"Statement by Alabama Clergymen, April 12, 1963"..........................142

"Letter from Birmingham Jail, April 16, 1963," by Martin Luther
King, Jr. 145

    Exercise Five 171

181 Chapter Six: Reviews and Other Expressions of Opinion

    "Medium Women: A Review of a Musical Version of *Little Women*,"
by Bill McMahon 182

    Exercise One 185

"Spaminator: A Review of *Spamalot: The Musical*," by Bill McMahon 187

    Exercise Two 190

    Writing Opportunity One 192

"Science and Religion: An Evolution Sunday Sermon, March 2, 2008," by
Rev. Scotty McLennan..193

    Exercise Three...202

205 Chapter Seven: Memoirs and Personal Essays

    "Mrs. Shelley to Mrs. [Maria] Gisborne," by Mary Shelley...................206

    Exercise One 220

"Surviving the Author Photo," by Matthew Pearl 222

    Exercise Two 226

    Writing Opportunity One 227

229 Chapter Eight: Common Logical Fallacies and Propaganda Techniques

Logical Fallacies..229

    Exercise One 234

Propaganda..236

    Exercise Two 244

INTRODUCTION:
HOW TO USE THIS BOOK

Reading and Analyzing Nonfiction: Slant, Spin, and Bias is a book that will help your students understand that virtually every writer—even the reporter who claims only to be providing information—has a purpose, an angle. Further, this book will help your students become familiar with the conventions and devices writers use to achieve their purposes. It describes how all writers, from the diarist to the propagandist, apply a degree of slant, spin, and sometimes outright bias to advance their points. Articles, letters, and speeches—both contemporary and classic—each annotated and accompanied by a thought-provoking exercise, will ensure your students' understanding and test their ability to recognize and distinguish among the various devices nonfiction writers employ.

Frequent writing prompts provide your students with the opportunity to hone their skills and apply the conventions they've been studying in their own writing.

This book is somewhat unique among textbooks in that, although the chapters are numbered, they are not necessarily written to be used sequentially. As the *genre* of nonfiction is so broad, and the characteristics of the various *subgenres* overlap to such a great extent, there is no need to study the news article before the memoir or *vice versa*.

Thus, if your need is simply to locate some excellent examples of nonfiction literature, this book can certainly be a worthwhile resource for you—even if you choose not to avail yourself of the exercise questions and writing opportunities.

If, however, your objectives include analyzing the interplay of rhetoric, logic, and emotion in the creation of nonfiction, then you will find the second chapter, which defines the key terms "slant," "spin," and "bias," and the final chapter, which defines and illustrates the most common logical fallacies and techniques of propaganda, to be particularly helpful.

In every chapter—in our discussion of each subgenre—we have followed a simple model-guided-practice-independent work process. The footnotes and margin annotations are intended to help guide your students to an independent analysis, and eventual evaluation, of what they have read.

We are confident, therefore, that you will find this book helpful in an Advanced Placement Language and Composition course, a general literature course that must include nonfiction, even a writing course in which you wish to give your students models to analyze and follow.

Reading and Analyzing Nonfiction: Slant, Spin, and Bias is intended to be a versatile book, adaptable to your specific needs and objectives. Begin at page one and lead your students through, or begin with the last chapter and skip around at will; allow the following selections to amuse your students, anger your students, or make them nod their heads in agreement. Our goal simply has been to provide you with excellent selections, both classic and contemporary, and enough guidance to help your students become careful, thoughtful readers.

ACKNOWLEDGMENTS

"A New Ice Age Is Coming - Movie Title Or Reality?" by Joseph LaStella, San Diego, California, 1 July, 2004 —/E-Wire/. Permission pending.

"Half-Baked Alaska." From *The New York Times*, © July 30, 2008, *The New York Times*. All rights reserved. Used by permission and protected by the Copyright Laws of the United States. The printing, copying, redistribution, or retransmission of the Material without express written permission is prohibited.

"Grant and Lee: A Study in Contrasts," by Bruce Catton. Excerpted from *The American Story* edited by Earl Schenck Miers. Copyright © Earl Schenck Miers. Reprinted with permission from the United States Capitol Historical Society.

"Destination America: Mount Rushmore," © 2006 by Tony Perrottet. Reprinted by permission of the author." Originally appeared in SMITHSONIAN (May 2006).

"All the Lonely People," by Rick Attig and Doug Bates. Copyright 2005 by OREGONIAN PUBG CO. Reproduced with permission of OREGONIAN PUBG CO. in the format Textbook via Copyright Clearance Center.

"One Flew Out of the Cuckoo's Nest," by Rick Attig and Doug Bates. Copyright 2005 by OREGONIAN PUBG CO. Reproduced with permission of OREGONIAN PUBG CO. in the format Textbook via Copyright Clearance Center.

"A Mad and Mindless Health Policy," by Rick Attig and Doug Bates. Copyright 2005 by OREGONIAN PUBG CO. Reproduced with permission of OREGONIAN PUBG CO. in the format Textbook via Copyright Clearance Center.

"Battle of the Babies" was first published in *Essays in Miniature*, by Agnes Repplier (Charles L. Webster & Co., 1892).

"A Call for Unity: Statement by Alabama Clergymen." Reprinted by arrangement with The Heirs to the Estate of Martin Luther King, Jr., c/o Writers House as agent for the proprietor New York, NY. *Copyright © 1963 Dr. Martin Luther King, Jr.; copyright © renewed 1991 Coretta Scott King.*

"Letter from Birmingham Jail." Reprinted by arrangement with The Heirs to the Estate of Martin Luther King, Jr., c/o Writers House as agent for the proprietor New York, NY. *Copyright © 1963 Dr. Martin Luther King, Jr.; copyright © renewed 1991 Coretta Scott King.*

"Medium Women: A Review of a Musical Version of *Little Women*," by Bill McMahon Copyright © Bill McMahon, 2005. Reprinted with permission of the author.

"Spaminator: A Review of *Spamalot: The Musical*," by Bill McMahon, Copyright © Bill McMahon, 2005. Reprinted with permission of the author.

"Science and Religion." From Scotty McLennan, *Jesus Was a Liberal*, published 2009, Palgrave Macmillan, reproduced with permission of Palgrave Macmillan.

"Mrs. Shelley to Mrs. [Maria] Gisborne," by Mary Shelley, from: Marshall, Julian, Mrs. *The life & letters of Mary Wollstonecraft Shelley* (Volume 2). London: Richard Bentley and Son, 1889.

"Surviving the Author Photo," by Matthew Pearl. Reprinted by permission of the author. All rights reserved. Photographs by Warren Pearl (2003), Beth Kelly (2003), and Sigrid Estrada (2006). Reproduced by permission of Matthew Pearl. All rights reserved.

Chapter One
WHAT IS NONFICTION?

The entire realm of literature—in all media: print, film, digital, electronic, or even media that haven't been discovered yet—can be divided into two broad categories or genres: fiction and nonfiction. Nonfiction is probably best defined, as it is named, in terms of what it is *not*. Nonfiction is *not fiction*.

Fiction is created. It is made up. It might incorporate historical, scientific, or some other type of fact, but if one single character is created by the author, if a single event is not documented as having happened, if a single line of dialogue is made up and is not an attempt to approximate what is known to have been said, then the literature in question is fiction.

Nonfiction is not fiction. It is not intentionally created by the author.

Does that mean nonfiction is factual? Not necessarily. The writer of a memoir or autobiography is writing from memory. What he or she remembers only vaguely cannot be called "factual." Compare multiple eyewitness accounts of the same incident. Each account is likely to be different from all the others in some way. The witnesses will probably even disagree on basic facts—physical descriptions, time of day, etc. Yet, unless one or more of the witnesses is intentionally creating his or her account, the accounts are nonfiction—even if they are not precisely factual.

But isn't nonfiction supposed to be "true"? Not necessarily. The author of an editorial is stating his or her opinion, and it is pointless to talk about the "truth" or "untruth" of an opinion. The same is true of a review of a movie, book, or play. Reviews are largely informed by the personal taste of the reviewer. Can one person's personal taste be "true" while another's is "false"?

Nonfiction is simply not fiction. Whatever its topic, its author is not intentionally creating the events, characters, settings. Whether the piece you're reading is a fact-filled article in a scientific journal, an emotional first-person account of a harrowing experience, or a loving tribute to one's grandparents, as long as the author is not intentionally creating the details, it is nonfiction.

Chapter Two

THE ELEMENTS OF NONFICTION

It still might be useful to define nonfiction in terms of what it *is*, in terms of its elements; for, like prose fiction, drama, and poetry, nonfiction is essentially the working together of certain elements.

> **Fact:** A fact is any statement that can be verified as true. One's knowledge or ignorance of a fact does not alter that fact. What one does with his or her knowledge of a fact does not alter the fact. A fact, by definition, is indisputable.

Facts can be as finite as a person's age, height, or weight; the date, time of day, or weather during a given event; or the measurable results of a test, survey, poll, etc.

Remember, however, that the presence of facts—or their accuracy—is not necessarily the *first* element of nonfiction; as we discussed above, it is the absence of creation that defines nonfiction.

> **Analysis of Fact:** There are entire college and graduate-school courses devoted to methods of gathering facts. Even your high school research projects have probably included instruction in gathering facts. Rarely, however, is it appropriate simply to report facts ("raw data"). Most of the time, the people who have gathered the facts will examine their data and then translate it into terms more understandable—and probably more interesting—to a broader audience. Note that analysis is not interpretation; the gatherers and reporters will not tell their audience what the data means, they will simply find more convenient ways to look at and talk about the data.

For example, the Constitution requires that the federal government conduct a census of the entire United States every ten years. Imagine that the census takers find the following (the following numbers are *not* really facts, they have been chosen to make the comparison between raw data and analysis easier to see):

RAW DATA

1,000,000 (1 million) people live in the United States.

700,000 (700 thousand) are gray.

200,000 (200 thousand) are green.

50,000 (50 thousand) are yellow.

40,000 (40 thousand) are blue.

10,000 (10 thousand) are transparent.

500,000 (500 thousand) people live in cities.

400,000 (400 thousand) live in suburban developments and/or small towns.

100,000 (100 thousand) live on farms.

350,000 (350 thousand) city dwellers are gray.

80,000 (80 thousand) city dwellers are green.

40,000 (40 thousand) city dwellers are yellow.

20,000 (20 thousand) city dwellers are blue.

10,000 (10 thousand) city dwellers are transparent.

The census gatherers could keep presenting these numbers, and eventually, your eyes would glaze over and you'd stop breathing (if you haven't already). If you wanted to write an article on the results of the most recent census, you'd want this information in a more useable form.

For example:

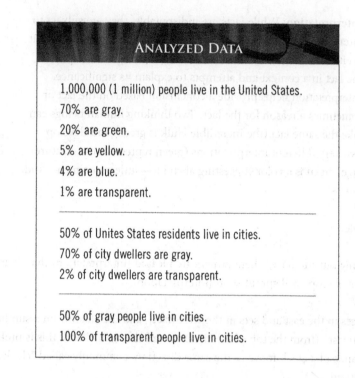

ANALYZED DATA

1,000,000 (1 million) people live in the United States.
70% are gray.
20% are green.
5% are yellow.
4% are blue.
1% are transparent.

50% of Unites States residents live in cities.
70% of city dwellers are gray.
2% of city dwellers are transparent.

50% of gray people live in cities.
100% of transparent people live in cities.

Notice that changing the numbers into percentages *does not change the facts at all*. Gray people are still 700,000 people out of a total of 1 million. They are still 10,000 out of 500,000 city dwellers. 10,000 transparent people out of a total of 10,000 transparent people live in cities. Presenting these numbers in percentages instead of raw numbers simply states the same information in terms that are easier to understand.

This is what analysis does: the information is translated into a variety of different formats, *but the information is not changed*. In fact, as long as the analysis is based on sound data (the census takers collected all of the forms and counted them accurately), the analysis can be treated as fact itself (but there are times when you'll want the data to support the analysis).

The analyst, however, does not tell you *what to think* of the fact that all of the transparent people in the United States live in cities.

That is *interpretation*.

> **Interpretation**: While facts are indisputable, they are subject to
> interpretation. Interpretation does not alter what a fact means (it
> is either raining outside, or it is not), but interpretation places
> the fact in a context and attempts to explain its significance.
> Interpretation helps provide a conclusion based on the fact or
> sometimes a reason for the fact. Two thinking human beings can
> take the same fact (the Incredible Hulk is green) and develop
> two very different interpretations (green represents the creature's
> rage; green is a color suggesting alien life—little green men—and
> illness).

For example:

If it is raining outside [fact], then farmers are pleased [interpretation] that their
newly-planted crops will sprout soon [interpretation].

The sun rises in the east and sets in the west [fact], and the shadow on a sundial
moves "sunwise" (from the top of the circle toward the right) [fact]; this is probably
why the hands of a clock move in the same direction, commonly called "clockwise"
[interpretation].

Interpretation is the basis of much nonfiction as the author of the editorial, review,
biography, or memoir will most likely take the facts of his or her subject and lead the
reader to a desired interpretation.

EXERCISE ONE:

Below are several statements. Identify each as either a verifiable fact or an interpretation. For each interpretation, speculate what fact is likely being interpreted.

1. Typically, only ___% of Americans eligible to vote actually do.

_____

_____

2. Americans have grown largely cynical and apathetic.

_____

_____

3. Several organizations exist to encourage non-registered voters to register and vote.

_____

_____

4. They have not been overly successful.

_____

_____

5. The moon cycles from new to full to new through a twenty-eight-day cycle.

_____

_____

6. The melody to which *The Star Spangled Banner* is sung was originally an English drinking song.

_____

_____

7. *The Star-Spangled Banner* was adopted as the United States' national anthem by a congressional resolution in 1931.

_____

_____

8. *America the Beautiful* was another song under consideration.

_____

_____

9. *The Star-Spangled Banner* was more beloved.

_____

_____

10. The song is a celebration of war and conquest.

_____

_____

> **Opinion**: Fact is verifiable. Interpretation is a conclusion based on fact or an assertion that can be supported by facts. Opinion is purely personal and can be completely subjective. One might have facts underlying his or her opinion, or there might be no factual or logical basis for the opinion at all.

That the sky is blue is a fact. That the sky is *pretty* is an opinion.

That ____% of all eligible voters actually vote is a verifiable fact. That this is due to American cynicism and apathy is an interpretation. That it is *deplorable that so few Americans vote* is an opinion.

Editorials, letters to the editor, and many blogs are based on the opinion of the writer. The writer of a memoir is likely to share his or her opinion of other people or events.

EXERCISE TWO:

Below are several statements. Identify each as either a verifiable fact, interpretation, or opinion. For each interpretation, speculate what fact is likely being interpreted. For each opinion, explain why it is opinion and not interpretation, and state whether there might be any factual basis for the opinion.

1. High tide at the beach is much more fun than low tide.

   _____

   _____

   _____

2. The phenomenon of high and low tide is a combination of the effects of the earth's rotation, the gravitational pull of the moon, and wind.

   _____

   _____

   _____

3. One would expect high tide to be higher than normal on nights when there is a full moon and the wind is blowing toward the shore.

   _____

   _____

   _____

4. People who own beachfront homes should take extra precautions on such nights to prevent floods.

   _____

   _____

   _____

5. The phases of the moon affect the cycle of high and low tides.

   _____

   _____

   _____

6. The "new moon," when the stars are not drowned out by moonlight, is the most beautiful phase.

_____

_____

_____

7. All beachfront property should be seized from private owners and turned into public recreational land.

_____

_____

_____

8. Because of potential damage due to floods and storms, beachfront property is expensive to insure.

_____

_____

_____

9. Global climate change is contributing to more frequent and more severe ocean storms.

_____

_____

_____

10. Global climate change has nothing to do with the current incidence of severe tropical storms.

_____

_____

_____

EXERCISE THREE:

Read the following excerpts from an online article about global climate change. For each numbered and underlined statement, identify whether the statement is fact/ analysis, interpretation, or opinion. Then, explain briefly why you believe as you do.

(1) <u>Scientists estimate</u> that (2) <u>Global Warming may cause two thirds of</u> China's Himalayan glaciers to melt by mid-century placing at least 300 million people at risk in China alone. (3) <u>"Of China's 1.3 billion people, 23 percent live around glaciers in the western part of the country</u> for the rich water resources they provide" (release from People's Daily Online). Himalayan glaciers feed seven great rivers of Asia that run through China and India, the world's most populous Nations, ensuring a year round water supply.

In January 2004, according to a recent scientific study published in the prestigious Scientific Journal Nature, (4) <u>"between 15 and 37 percent of the world's species may face extinction by 2050 due to Global Warming."</u> In one of the biggest mass extinctions since the demise of the dinosaurs, (5) <u>this loss could total 1.25 million species.</u> The Report's Authors are calling for a "rapid implementation of technologies" to combat the human causes of climate changes.

U.S. Pentagon researchers have concluded that as the planet warms, drastic changes in weather will result in worldwide ecosystems changes, which in turn will cause massive political and social instability.

And finally from the L.A. Times article (June 28, 2004) entitled "Early Snowmelt Ignites Global Warming Worries": (6) <u>"The Sierra snow pack appears to be melting earlier,</u> while another major water source, the Colorado River, is in (7) <u>a drought that appears to be the region's worst since 1590 to 1594, according to the U.S. Geological Survey."</u>

The Sierra snow pack includes three mountain ranges: Sierra, Cascade and Rocky that provide the bulk of the water supply to Western United States. The Western States and U.S. farmers are at great risk with enormous concern about this Global Warming Event.

. . .

An article by Brad Lemley, published in Discover Magazine (September 2002), clearly outlines this scenario: "The Gulf Stream, which warms both North America and Europe, could be affected by this trend causing a fall of the northern penetration of Gulf Stream waters. The freshwater mass that is accumulating now could shut down the entire system favoring conditions for a 'mini-Ice Age' that

➤ can last for 300-500 years (a typical Ice Age would last for thousands of years)."

What is a mini-Ice Age? To understand this we must visualize a real Ice Age. During the past Ice Age, which ended about 10,000 years ago, New York City was covered with an ice sheet several thousand feet thick! (8) <u>Even a so-called mini-Ice Age would be devastating!</u>

What can we do, while the politicians argue about Global Warming? We as citizens can do a lot and we can do it without asking anyone's permission.

One of the major causes of Global Warming is CO2 emissions, which is a product of burning anything—i.e. oil, gas, diesel, wood and even the fuel to power electric, hybrid, and hydrogen-powered cars.

Fact: The average American automobile releases into the atmosphere 80 pounds of CO2 for each 100 miles it is driven. Even a drive to the supermarket will produce several pounds of CO2 emissions. Our atmosphere is not a free sewer and is very fragile. Comparison: If the Earth were the size of a bowling ball, a layer thinner than a sheet of paper would be the equivalent "breathable atmosphere" around it.

(9) <u>The only practical way to cut CO2 emissions is to stop burning fuel</u>, energy conservation or to utilize renewable energy and fuels, which some believe will slow down our industrial growth. That is why our current administration in Washington has refused to sign the Kyoto Protocol, which has already been signed by 166 nations.

The Kyoto Treaty states that the nations of the world must reduce CO2 emissions to 8% below their 1990 level by the year 2012.

The European Union (EU) and many other nations have already begun to reduce their CO2 emissions. The United States presently produces 25% of the entire CO2 emissions on the planet. However, without a policy change the U.S. will increase CO2 emissions by 35% by 2020. For example, the United States presently uses 70 percent more energy per million dollars generated by the economy than the European Union. The EU'S greenhouse gas emissions are down 4% from 1990 levels and the U.S. emissions are up 11%. It is time to join the rest of the world in the urgent need to clean up the environment.

(10) <u>The EU has recently taken great steps to further reduce its CO2 emissions</u> and dependence on foreign oil by increasing alternative fuel production.

. . .

(from Joseph P. LaStella, P.E. "A New Ice Age Is Coming - Movie Title Or Reality?" San Diego, California, 1 July, 2004 —/E-Wire/. Permission pending.)

1. _____
   _____
   _____
   _____

2. _____
   _____
   _____
   _____

3. _____
   _____
   _____
   _____

4. _____
   _____
   _____
   _____

5. _____
   _____
   _____
   _____

6. _____
   _____
   _____
   _____

7. _____

_____

_____

_____

8. _____

_____

_____

_____

9. _____

_____

_____

_____

10. _____

_____

_____

_____

Chapter Three
SLANT, SPIN, AND BIAS

So far, we've looked fairly objectively at the elements from which nonfiction writers build their articles, editorials, memoirs, or whatever. These elements are, essentially, outside of the writer and do not necessarily indicate the writer's personality or values. Writers, however, rarely write with *only* the intent of sharing information or helping to break down enormous volumes of information into digestible bits. It is not unfair to say that most writers—whether they be reporters or memoirists—have a purpose—a point they hope to establish, a view they hope to support, a value they hope to spread.

The fact that the writer has a purpose is not a bad thing. Without author's purpose, all writing would be bland fact and interpretation. Some writers' purposes, however, are more innocent than others, and some writers are more honest in communicating their purposes to their readers. It is because, as the educated citizenry of a free nation, we have the right to explore issues and formulate our own views that we need to be aware of how some writers simply want to help inform our views, while others may actually intend to shape our views for us.

All writers select the people they intend to write for, and all writers select the information they will share with those readers. All nonfiction, therefore, exhibits the qualities of **slant**, **spin**, and **bias** to some extent. The key to reading to be informed instead of indoctrinated, therefore, is knowing to expect at least some manipulation of the facts, recognizing the extent to which legitimate information has been manipulated, and being able to look beyond the writer's work to the underlying information.

Let's begin by defining the terms:

> **SLANT**: Virtually nothing that is written is written without slant. From your earliest writing experiences, you have probably been taught to consider your audience, to include only those facts and details that your audience will need to follow your point, to choose words and sentence structures appropriate for your intended audience's age and level of education. At its simplest and most innocent, slant is little more than a writer's awareness of audience.

At some point in your writing instruction, you have probably also been taught to consider the *purpose* of what you're writing. Is your intent merely to inform, to share facts? Is your purpose actually to persuade your readers to change their viewpoint or behavior? Are you writing a "feel-good" piece intended to affirm what your readers already believe, or are you hoping to challenge the conventional wisdom? This awareness of purpose will also govern the facts you include and the extent to which you explain, define, and interpret those facts. Adherence to purpose, then, is also an innocent aspect of slant.

Since all writers are taught to keep audience and purpose in mind for everything except their most personal writing, there is very little nonfiction that you will read that is not slanted in one direction or another. Readers tend to be more accepting of articles slanted *toward their own* values, beliefs, and experience than they are of articles slanted *away from* them; but slant alone does not discredit a piece or its writer as long as the writer is candid in acknowledging his or her audience and purpose.

Consider the following op-ed[1] piece that appeared in the *New York Times* and notice the clues that suggest the author's audience and purpose.

---

1 *"Op-ed" is the common name of the page in the newspaper opposite the editorial page. It usually contains readers' letters to the editor and guest columns.*

HALF-BAKED ALASKA
BY TOBY BARLOW

Looking in the mirror, I saw Gopher. That didn't feel so good.

For the record, the only reason my friends and I had ever watched *The Love Boat* was that the VCR hadn't been invented yet and we were stuck with just the three networks. So while our parents were downstairs with their cocktails and dinner parties, we stared glumly at the show with an ever-growing awareness of just how awful it was.

But less than 10 years later I, like Gregor Samsa before me, experienced a metamorphic transformation—into Gopher.

That summer, I somehow became the chief steward on a cruise ship that traveled along the coast of southeastern Alaska up into Glacier Bay, and every morning I slapped on my itchy 60/40 polyester shirt and slacks, a name tag reading "Toby" and a queasy, saccharine smile.

Alaska wasn't supposed to be like this. Inspired by visions of Jack London and Jack Kerouac, I had hitched, bused and boated north to spend that college summer "roughing it." My friend Marshall had roughed it the summer before, and returned with tales of muddy cannery camps filled with hard labor and free love. So I packed my duffel (not very well), gathered my money

The very short first paragraph with an allusion to a popular 1970s television character, plus the absence of anything like a thesis, suggests that the author's purpose is to entertain. The nature of the allusion suggests that he is writing for an older, adult audience.

By explaining the earlier allusion, the author broadens his audience, but it is still apparent that he is writing to adults.

The mildly cantankerous tone also suggests that the author's purpose is other than to persuade or to inform.

Another allusion, this one to literature, clearly establishes the author's intended audience as somewhat educated adults.

Having established his audience, the author continues with the allusions.

The tongue-in-cheek tone, reinforced by the parallel parenthetical side comments, reinforces our understanding that the author's purpose is to entertain and not persuade or inform.

Even after the author has established the basic allusion to the 1970s television show, *The Love Boat*, it is clear that he is excluding from his intended audience anyone who will not understand the references to these actors and the format of the show.

The quotation is probably made up but reflective of the types of comments the passengers made. The author is mocking the passengers.

(not very much) and set out from New Mexico for the Last Frontier.

A month later, my lousy planning, poor decision-making and some grotesque prevarications had landed me on this low-rent version of the Pacific Princess. The tourists were eerily similar to Ruth Buzzi, Tom Bosley and the other "special guest stars" of the show. As long as there was a glacier or a shore full of puffins to point at with their bulky camcorders, they were happy. Otherwise, they all seemed unsure of what they were supposed to do. "Where are the puffins?" the passengers would demand, "Where are the puffins!"

But the serene landscape of Alaska never ceased to amaze me. Immense mountains soared up from the narrow fjords and disappeared into the wispy dreamlike clouds above. Bald eagles circled overhead. I just didn't get to see much of it. Odds were, when we finally reached a picturesque site like the puffin-filled shores of Willoughby Island, I would be crouched over in the dark, airless supply closet, carefully counting boxes of plastic spoons.

We boiled enormous cans of industrial soup and served it in fancy bowls along with cheese and cheap, salty meats. We fished blue glacial ice out of the bay to drop into the drinks and doubled the price. The passengers often seemed uneasy. They felt they were being had, but what could they do? They were stuck on the boat, just like me.

I could not get over the fact that I was supposed to be somewhere else, elbow deep in fish guts, singing rowdy camp songs with worldly, well-read cannery workers and, ideally, voluptuous co-eds. But weeks before, when I had first reached Juneau, the canneries were still 900 miles away and I had only $30 left in my pocket. Stepping into the Alaska state employment office was my only choice.

There I earnestly answered the curt state worker's questions: "Age?" 19. "Experience?" Not a lot. "References?" None. He looked me over, clearly unimpressed. He mentioned there might be some day labor moving dry wall. I could wait and see if it came in.

Amid the gray file cabinets, the fake wood paneling and the buzzing fluorescent lights, I had a sinking feeling that the Jack London and Jack Kerouac portion of my trip had just run aground.

> Notice how the author reiterates his allusion to London and Kerouac, to contrast their writing with his current experience. Note also the pun that emphasizes the tongue-in-cheek tone of the entire piece.

As I chatted with the other would-be day laborers, someone mentioned that a new cruise ship was hiring. Someone else knew the hotel suite where the interviews were being conducted.

All I knew about cruise ship work was what I'd once seen Julie, Isaac and Gopher do, which wasn't much. But by the time I reached that hotel suite and met the recruiter, I had plenty of relevant experience. "Age?" 22! "Experience?" Tons! Waiter, head waiter, assistant manager, you name it! "References?" Sure! Imaginary names and phone numbers spilled out. Figuring that nobody would bother checking references from distant East Coast time zones, I was as brazen as I could be.

> Here he reiterates, and expands upon, his original allusion.

I did a good job with my lies, too good a job, because within 48 hours I was overseeing the daytime staff of stewards along with a bartender named Bobby. I was expected to manage the inventory and back up Bobby when we got in the weeds. I was also, in the words of the recruiter, expected to "inspire the crew."

That was a challenge. The crew members seemed to sense I didn't belong there. Or perhaps I was just being paranoid. Or perhaps they could sense my paranoia. In any case, they steered clear of me, growing listless and far from inspired.

Consequently, at a fairly good rate, one or two would miss the boat, leading to their immediate dismissal ("Bye, Bobby!") and leaving me vacuuming or folding napkins or filling in the gaps however I could. We were regularly understaffed and I was generally overwhelmed, busily filling the salt shakers and clearing the tables, scampering off to get the captain his coffee and rearranging the deck chairs.

When I collapsed at the end of the day, the exhaustion wasn't the satisfying sort from enduring hard, physical labor but rather the frazzled, nervous fatigue you get when you've taken too many margarita orders from shrill groups of excited retirees, the sort who think you're "the nicest boy." Disappointment stuck to me the same way that oily, oozy sweat seeped into my uniform's polyester mix.

Sure, I sensed that the idyllic salmon camps of my dreams probably didn't exist and that fish gutting was most likely laborious, tiresome and mind-numbing. But I couldn't see that. I could see only how my lies had served me up a punishment I deserved, a service industry purgatory worse than any frozen yogurt shop in any mall on earth.

I began to recognize too that the sad, grotesque picture I painted of the tourists was childish and cynical. We all had come a great distance, but they had gotten here honestly. In the end they were simply decent people spending a lot of hard-earned money who earnestly wanted to believe it was worth it.

My entire journey had been a test, one that I had completely failed, proving only that I was made of low and dishonorable stuff. Sitting in the galley, putting on my nametag and getting ready to face another round of customers, I had to admit that, compared with me, Gopher was a real man.

Even though the tone is beginning to shift to a more serious and reflective one, there is still no thesis to support that the author is arguing a point. His essential purpose has not yet changed.

The shift in tone includes a change in how he recalls his passengers. Remember that the audience he is apparently writing for is very similar to these passengers.

Toby Barlow is the author of Sharp Teeth.

Notice that there is nothing terribly questionable or controversial about this *New York Times* op-ed piece, but the author clearly identifies that he is writing to a fairly specific audience—essentially people around his own age and level of education and experience. This is made most apparent by his choice of allusions—which he does not belabor with long and detailed explanations for persons *not* in his intended audience. This column, then, is slanted toward a middle-class, middle-aged audience.

Most magazines and newspapers (not to mention blogs, listserves, and e-zines) are slanted to a particular audience: pre-teen girls; single, twenty-something New Yorkers; young parents, etc. There is not necessarily anything wrong or misleading about a writer's selecting facts and details most relevant to his or her audience, using language that is going to be most clear to that audience, and being consistent in his or her intent to persuade, inform, or entertain that intended audience. These are the choices virtually every author makes in virtually every piece he or she writes.

Other types of language and information manipulation, however, become somewhat more problematic.

> **SPIN**: Two well-known adages address the idea of spin: "There are two sides to every story" and "every cloud has a silver lining." The first addresses a very legitimate purpose served by writers of nonfiction: to provide information that might alter the reader's perception of a person or issue. The second addresses the stereotypical role of a "spin doctor": to present a negative issue in as positive light as possible. The corollary to the second adage might be "Every silver lining has a cloud," which addresses a writer's desire to de-emphasize the positive qualities and accomplishments of his or her opponent.

Spin, then, is a fairly new term that has its roots in a fairly old concept: to "spin" a yarn (to fabricate a tale). At its most innocent, spin is little more than a severe slant—a focus on the facts, data, and examples that support a single interpretation. At its most dangerous, spin can come very close to propaganda and outright deception.

Still, one should not absolutely reject a written piece simply because there is an apparent spin to the facts presented. The reader who is aware of the spin can read past it and discern whatever useful information is to be gained from the piece. Plus, the spin might legitimately be simply an examination of the "other side of the coin" or the "silver lining of the cloud."

Some brief examples of "two sides to every story" spin could include:

The fact that, on last year's state assessment, 58% of all tenth-graders in the district are reading at or above grade level means that

(-) 42% are still reading *below* grade level.

(+) considering the previous year's findings of 52% below grade level, the district has made *significant gains* in its attempts to improve reading instruction.

Record-setting amounts of snow in the Midwest have

(-) caused hundreds of thousands of dollars of damage and left hundreds of rural residents stranded without access to emergency services.

(+) replenished the wells and reservoirs that had reached dangerously low levels after several years of drought.

The first example tells the "other side of the story." In the late twentieth and early twenty-first centuries, it has become very popular in the United States to derogate the public education system, and many public officials like to seize upon statistics like the 42% to "prove" the school system's failure. Others prefer to place the current statistic into some kind of context and attempt to forecast a trend. If the "reading at or above grade level rate" had gone *down*, no amount of spin would have made the report look like good news. But an *increase* might indicate that the school is on the right track and should continue its current program for another year or two to see whether the statistics continue to improve.

The second example illustrates the "silver lining" spin.

What is important to note is that, in *neither* case is the writer trying to deceive the reader. All of the conclusions are valid; each one simply illustrates the writer's desire to lead the reader to a desired negative or positive conclusion.

There are times, however, when the spin's intent is to deceive, or at least to draw the reader's attention away from an opposing viewpoint. An excessive use of euphemisms or exaggerations, for example, is a clue to the possibility of deceit. When a shipwreck or an oil spill becomes an "incident," the spin doctor's intent is more to deceive than to highlight the positive. Similarly, when a radical group calls a relatively minor mishap a "disaster," the exaggeration is clearly intended to deceive more than suggest a reasonable interpretation.

Here are two accounts from two different newspapers about the same event. Notice how each is spun to lead its readers to a particular conclusion. Pay attention to information that is verifiable fact, what is interpretation, and what may actually be opinion masquerading as fact or interpretation.

OFFICER ASSAULTED WHILE INVESTIGATING HOME INVASION

SEASIDE, AZ, 2 June 2009—While responding to a routine complaint Monday afternoon, Seaside Police Sergeant Donald Oates was shocked to find himself verbally and physically assaulted by the man whose home and property he'd been called to protect.

"Sure it was a misunderstanding," Oates said in a telephone interview, "but we had received a legitimate concern, and we had an obligation to check it out."

The "legitimate concern" was a telephone call at 1:37 Monday afternoon from Beachfront Drive resident Alitta Noazie reporting that someone was "breaking down" her next-door-neighbor's front door. "I knew he was out of town," Noazie said, "and I don't want this to become the kind of neighborhood where people don't look out for each other."

Sergeant Oates, a twenty-three-year veteran of the department, arrived to find the front door of 11234 Beachfront Drive wide open and what he described as a "mean, surly-looking man pawing through a bunch of bags on the floor in the hallway." According to Oates's official report, when he asked the man to identify himself and state his reason for being in the house, the intruder—who turned out to be the home's owner, Professor Jeremiah Hargrove—ignored the request and continued "pawing" through the bags.

Place and time of the incident are verifiable facts, as are the identities of the persons involved.

To call an exchange an "assault" is an interpretation.

That the neighbor called is a fact. That someone was breaking in is an interpretation.

The reporter probably includes this detail to establish Oates's reliability and credibility.

That this is his description is a fact. The actual description ("mean, surly-looking") is opinion.

"All he had to do was tell me his name," Oates insisted. "Instead, he demanded to know my name and badge number, and he kept messing with his bags." Oates's report asserts that, when he placed his hand on the intruder's shoulder in order to attract his attention, Hargrove stood up and made a move as if to strike the officer. To protect himself, Oates reports that he held the man at arm's length and again requested that he identify himself.

"But he moved again toward the bag, so I cuffed him and escorted him to my car. It wasn't until his arraignment yesterday that I found out who he was."

Once it was established that no home invasion had taken place, all charges against Professor Hargrove were dropped. He has elected not to press any charges against either the arresting officer or the Seaside Police Department. The incident is being investigated by the Seaside Police Department's Internal Affairs Division, but it is clear that Sergeant Oates followed all approved procedures in the incident.

Notice how this part of the incident is reported in the other article. What facts can you infer from the two reports?

Here is an example of an opinion masquerading as a fact. Whether or not Oates followed police procedure will be determined by the investigation. To say that "it is clear" that he did suggests a conclusion that has not been established yet.

HOMECOMING MARRED BY POLICE HARASSMENT

SEASIDE, AZ, 2 June 2009—What was to have been Professor Jeremiah Hargrove's long-anticipated return from an international lecture tour turned ugly when local police, responding to a report of an attempted break-in, repeatedly struck the 78-year-old expert on Constitutional Law, forcing him to the floor, and handcuffing him before dragging him from his own home and into a waiting squad car.

Fact. They were responding to a report.

Just as the reporter in the previous article established that Oates was a twenty-three-year veteran, this reporter hopes to establish Hargrove's credibility—and possibly build reader sympathy for him as well.

"I was searching in my carry-on for my passport when the officer grabbed my hand," said the disgruntled Hargrove at his Tuesday-morning arraignment. "When I tried to free myself from the officer's restraint, he punched me in the stomach. And screamed at me to tell him my name."

That he said this is a fact. What he is saying is his interpretation of the events.

The incident started innocently enough. Professor Hargrove arrived at his home on Beachfront Drive and let himself into the house in which he has lived for twenty-five years. Because the front door sticks, according to Hargrove, he had to force it open with his shoulder. This is apparently what Hargrove's neighbor, Alitta Noazie, saw when she called the police to report a break-in in progress at her neighbor's home.

Opinion.

"Stormed" is a strong word. It is an interpretation of how the police entered, but it is an emotion-laden word.

This is tricky. That he said this is fact. His version of his actions is also fact but may not be true.

"Yelling" and "hitting" are Hargrove's interpretations of Oates's actions.

The decision is fact. Whether or not it is "magnanimous" is a matter of opinion.

This is clearly Hargrove's opinion. What effect is achieved by ending the article with this quotation?

When the officer stormed into his home—the front door was still open when Oates arrived—Hargrove says he reached for his passport in order to identify himself and prove that he was in his own home. "But the officer, who refused to identify himself, started yelling and hitting, and I never had the chance to show him my I.D. I was assaulted in my own home by the very person charged with protecting me in that home."

Seaside Police Officer Sergeant Donald Oates insists he followed appropriate protocols for responding to a report of a home invasion. The matter is under investigation by the Seaside Police Department's Internal Affairs Division. Professor Hargrove has magnanimously decided not to press criminal or civil charges against Sergeant Oates or the Seaside Police Department. "What good would it do, anyway?" he lamented. "We all know that lawyers and judges always side with the cops."

EXERCISE ONE:

Consider the following statements, pulled from the two articles. In the space provided, state whether each one is a fact, an interpretation, or an opinion.

If the statement is an interpretation, state the fact on which the interpretation is based. Then, explain whether the interpretation helps to spin the information in one direction or the other.

If the statement is an opinion, decide whether there is any factual basis for the opinion. Then, explain whether the interpretation helps to spin the information in one direction or the other.

1. verbally and physically assaulted

   intepertation; Mr. Hargrove said he was assaulted
   while Mr. Oates said he simply touched him
   and talked in a normal voice.
   _____
   _____

2. I don't want this to become the kind of neighborhood where people don't look out for each other.

   opinion; we don't Know if she meant it,
   or she doesn't WANT to be that neighbor
   _____
   _____
   _____

3. a twenty-three-year veteran of the department

   fact
   _____
   _____
   _____
   _____

4. Professor Jeremiah Hargrove ignored the request.

interpretation, Professor Jeremiah
Hargrove could have just not heard
the request.

5. dragging him from his own home

., he was pulled out but
the dragging was opinionated.

6. "When I tried to free myself from the officer's restraint, he punched me in the stomach. And screamed at me to tell him my name."

opinion masquerading as a
interpretation, the Proffessor thinks
this but the police did say that he
spoke and touched him but not
in this manner

7. in which he has lived for twenty-five years

fact

8. the front door sticks

interpretation, the front door could be interpretated into 2 ways, it does or it doesn't

fact

9. This is apparently what Hargrove's neighbor, Alitta Noazie, saw

opinion, this is what Alitta thinks she saw, but according to the Professor

interpretation

10. I never had the chance to show him my I.D.

opinion

BIAS: Everyone has an opinion, and everyone has a right to his or her opinion. It might even be argued that everyone has a right to state his or her own opinion, and, as we've already discussed, much of nonfiction is written with the express purpose of stating the writer's opinion.

So, there is nothing wrong with having an opinion or writing an editorial, letter to the editor, or blog to state that opinion. Bias, however, is considerably different. Both slant and spin acknowledge that there *are* other views, that there *are* facts that might cast the issue in a different light. Slant, and to perhaps a lesser degree spin, even tends to concede the possibility that there is some validity to these other views. Bias, however, is largely founded on the premise—whether conscious or not—that the facts presented are the *only* valid facts, that the thesis argued is the *only* tenable view, and that no other discussion is necessary—or even possible.

Biased pieces are often filled with errors in logic, careful application of rhetorical devices, and sometimes outright propaganda (see Chapter Eight).

Consider the following historical document. Many readers may actually be offended by the suggestion that the document is biased, but a close examination shows that the sole purpose of the document was to justify what the majority of the world would probably have condemned as immoral and illegal action. The writers are not inviting open discussion; they are having their say and clearly suggesting that there is no reasonable "other side of the story."

THE UNANIMOUS DECLARATION OF THE THIRTEEN UNITED STATES OF AMERICA

When, in the course of human events, it becomes necessary for one people to dissolve the political bonds which have connected them with another, and to assume among the powers of the earth, the separate and equal station to which the laws of nature and of nature's God entitle them, *a decent respect to the opinions of mankind* requires that they should declare the causes which impel them to the separation.

Considering that the three world powers at the time—England, France, and Spain—were all monarchies to one degree or another, there is absolutely no basis for this claim.

We hold these truths to be self-evident, that all men are created equal, that they are endowed by their Creator with certain unalienable rights, that among these are life, liberty and the pursuit of happiness. That to secure these rights, governments are instituted among men, *deriving their just powers from the consent of the governed.* That whenever any form of government becomes destructive to these ends, it is *the right of the people* to alter or to abolish it, and to institute new government, laying its foundation on such principles and organizing its powers in such form, as to them shall seem most likely to effect their safety and happiness. Prudence, indeed, will dictate that governments long established should not be changed for light and transient causes; and accordingly all experience hath shown that mankind are more disposed to suffer, while evils are sufferable, than to right themselves by abolishing the forms to which they

The "Self-Evident Truth" is a basic logical fallacy. The writer making such a claim either cannot conceive of someone's holding a different view or completely abdicates any responsibility to support the claim. There is no room for discussion or disagreement.

Again, this statement is being offered as a "Self-Evident Truth." And, given the time in which it was written, such a government, exercising "just powers" with the "consent" of the masses of people, did not exist—and had never existed.

Again, the concept of people's rights is essentially being invented. Even in countries like England in which "the people" enjoyed certain rights protected by law, "the people" did not include the poorest classes, women, or children.

Remember that all of these ideas are included under the "Self-Evident Truth" umbrella, so the writers claim there is no need to defend their assertion that "the people" have the "right" to "alter or abolish" their current government and institute a new one.

43

Such strong language borders on Name-Calling, another basic propaganda technique.

Pin-pointing the enemy, also called Scapegoating, is another propaganda technique. History shows that Parliament was no friend to the American colonies either, but that body is not blamed in this document. King George is given the full brunt of responsibility.

Each of the next thirteen statements, each set off as a separate paragraph, begins with the word "he" to emphasize the assertion that the fault lies with "the present King of Great Britain" and no one else. This rhetorical use of repetition is intended to drive the reader into passionate agreement.

are accustomed. But when a long train of abuses and usurpations, pursuing invariably the same object evinces a design to reduce them under *absolute despotism*, it is their right, it is their duty, to throw off such government, and to provide new guards for their future security. —Such has been the patient sufferance of these colonies; and such is now the necessity which constrains them to alter their former systems of government. The history of *the present King of Great Britain* is a history of repeated injuries and usurpations, all having in direct object the establishment of an absolute tyranny over these states. To prove this, let facts be submitted to a candid world.

He has refused his assent to laws, the most wholesome and necessary for the public good.

He has forbidden his governors to pass laws of immediate and pressing importance, unless suspended in their operation till his assent should be obtained; and when so suspended, he has utterly neglected to attend to them.

He has refused to pass other laws for the accommodation of large districts of people, unless those people would relinquish the right of representation in the legislature, a right inestimable to them and formidable to tyrants only.

He has called together legislative bodies at places unusual, uncomfortable, and distant from the depository of their public records, for the sole purpose of fatiguing them into compliance with his measures.

He has dissolved representative houses repeatedly, for opposing with manly firmness his invasions on the rights of the people.

He has refused for a long time, after such dissolutions, to cause others to be elected; whereby the legislative powers, incapable of annihilation, have returned to the people at large for their exercise; the state remaining in the meantime exposed to all the dangers of invasion from without, and convulsions within.

He has endeavored to prevent the population of these states; for that purpose obstructing the laws for naturalization of foreigners; refusing to pass others to encourage their migration hither, and raising the conditions of new appropriations of lands.

He has obstructed the administration of justice, by refusing his assent to laws for establishing judiciary powers.

He has made judges dependent on his will alone, for the tenure of their offices, and the amount and payment of their salaries.

He has erected a multitude of new offices, and sent hither swarms of officers to harass our people, and eat out their substance.

He has kept among us, in times of peace, standing armies without the consent of our legislature.

He has affected to render the military independent of and superior to civil power.

All of these allegations can be supported by at least one factual example, but the writers of this Declaration do not want their readers to have the opportunity to argue the "other side." They want only their side considered.

He has combined with others to subject us to a jurisdiction foreign to our constitution, and unacknowledged by our laws; giving his assent to their acts of pretended legislation:

For quartering large bodies of armed troops among us:

For protecting them, by mock trial, from punishment for any murders which they should commit on the inhabitants of these states:

For cutting off our trade with all parts of the world:

For imposing taxes on us without our consent:

For depriving us in many cases, of the benefits of trial by jury:

For transporting us beyond seas to be tried for pretended offenses:

For abolishing the free system of English laws in a neighboring province, establishing therein an arbitrary government, and enlarging its boundaries so as to render it at once an example and fit instrument for introducing the same absolute rule in these colonies:

For taking away our charters, abolishing our most valuable laws, and altering fundamentally the forms of our governments:

For suspending our own legislatures, and declaring themselves invested with power to legislate for us in all cases whatsoever.

He has abdicated government here, by declaring us out of his protection and waging war against us.

He has plundered our seas, ravaged our coasts, burned our towns, and destroyed the lives of our people.

He is at this time transporting large armies of foreign mercenaries to complete the works of death, desolation and tyranny, already begun with circumstances of cruelty and perfidy *scarcely paralleled in the most barbarous ages,* and totally unworthy the head of a civilized nation.

He has constrained our fellow citizens taken captive on the high seas to bear arms against their country, to become the executioners of their friends and brethren, or to fall themselves by their hands.

He has excited domestic insurrections amongst us, and has endeavored to bring on the inhabitants of our frontiers, the merciless Indian savages, whose known rule of warfare, is undistinguished destruction of all ages, sexes and conditions.

In *every stage of these oppressions we have petitioned for redress in the most humble terms*: our repeated petitions have been answered only by repeated injury. A prince, whose character is thus marked by every act which may define a tyrant, is unfit to be the ruler of a free people.

While not usually identified as a propaganda technique, exaggeration can be a very effective means of swaying another person's opinion—remember the earlier references to "absolute despotism" and "absolute tyranny." Also, the writers offer no specific examples, invite no discussion or disagreement.

More rhetorical exaggeration.

Again, the writers of the Declaration do not want the readers of this document to recall incidents like the Boston Tea Party, acts of intimidation committed by The Sons of Liberty, and so on. In this document, the Colonies must be blameless.

Nor have we been wanting in attention to our British brethren. We have warned them from time to time of attempts by their legislature to extend an unwarrantable jurisdiction over us. We have reminded them of the circumstances of our emigration and settlement here. We have appealed to their native justice and magnanimity, and we have conjured them by the ties of our common kindred to disavow these usurpations, which, would inevitably interrupt our connections and correspondence. They too have been deaf to the voice of justice and of consanguinity. We must, therefore, acquiesce in the necessity, which denounces our separation, and hold them, as we hold the rest of mankind, enemies in war, in peace friends.

Recall earlier references to "nature and nature's God" and the "Creator" by whom humankind's inalienable rights were bestowed. Whether the writers actually believed it, an appeal to this higher authority is another way for them--and possibly the reader, as well--to abdicate responsibility.

This is the Declaration of Independence, the actual message sent out to the world. Everything else serves merely to pacify resistance and preclude discussion.

We, therefore, the representatives of the United States of America, in General Congress, assembled, *appealing to the Supreme Judge of the world* for the rectitude of our intentions, do, *in the name, and by the authority of the good people of these colonies, solemnly publish and declare, that these united colonies are, and of right ought to be free and independent states; that they are absolved from all allegiance to the British Crown, and that all political connection between them and the state of Great Britain, is and ought to be totally dissolved; and that as free and independent states, they have full power to levy war, conclude peace, contract alliances, establish commerce, and to do all other acts and things which independent states may of right do.* And for the support of this declaration, with a firm reliance on the protection of Divine Providence, we mutually pledge to each other our lives, our fortunes and our sacred honor.

While a person's statement of opinion is usually obvious, bias is usually subtle, hidden. There are times, even, when the author is unaware that he or she has written a biased piece. This is one reason why bias is such a dangerous factor: the writer who genuinely cannot conceive of an opposing view can be very persuasive in his or her one-sidedness.

Take, for example, these editorials by the famous Arthur Brisbane. Granted, as editorials, they are statements of individual opinions and values, but careful readers and listeners will want to know the basis, factual and otherwise, of those opinions and values. The debate still continues whether the purpose of the news media (which today includes electronic sources as well as print and broadcast media) is to *shape* public opinion or merely to *reflect* it. Either way, a careful reader will want to make certain he or she is not nodding in agreement with biased views that might not stand up to open and honest discourse.

As you read the following, think about what Brisbane's theses are and how he goes about convincing his reader of the validity of these theses. How much of his editorial is founded in fact? How much interpretation of fact does he present? How much opinion?

What role do propaganda, logical fallacies, and rhetorical skill play in the editor's laying out his arguments?

WHY WOMEN SHOULD VOTE
BY ARTHUR BRISBANE

In this country and throughout the world women progress toward the full possession of the ballot, and toward equality with men in educational facilities. In one State after another women are beginning to practice law, they are obtaining new suffrage rights, they flock to newly opened schools and colleges.

These are probably facts—general, but factual.

In England and Scotland, but a few years ago, only a few men in the population were allowed to vote—money was the requisite quality. To-day, in those countries, women vote at county elections, and in many cases at municipal elections. In Utah, Colorado, and Idaho, women as voters have the same rights as men. They have certain rights as voters in nine other States. In the great Commonwealth of New Zealand, so far ahead of all the rest of the world in humanity and social progress, the wife votes absolutely as her husband does.

The voting laws of other nations and some states within the U.S. are easily verifiable.

The woman who votes becomes an important factor in life, for a double reason. In the first place, when a woman votes, the candidate must take care that his conduct and record meet with a good woman's approval, and this makes better men of the candidates.

Opinion.

This is an example of the logical fallacy called "begging the question." It is a conclusion based on an opinion that has been presented as established fact.

In the second place, and far more important, is this reason:

When women shall vote, the political influence of the good men in the community will be greatly increased. There is no doubt whatever that women, in their voting, will be influenced by the men whom they know. But there is also no doubt that they will be influenced by the GOOD men whom they know.

How similar is this claim to the "Self-Evident Truth"?

Men can deceive each other much more easily than they can deceive women—the latter being providentially provided with the X-ray of intuitional perception.

The blustering politician, preaching what he does not practice, may hold forth on the street corner or in a saloon, and influence the votes of others as worthless as himself. But among women his home life will more than offset his political influence.

The bad husband may occasionally get the vote of a deluded or frightened wife, but he will surely lose the votes of the wives and daughters next door.

Voting by women will improve humanity, because IT WILL COMPEL MEN TO SEEK AND EARN THE APPROVAL OF WOMEN.

Our social system improves in proportion as the men in it are influenced by its good women.

As for the education of women, it would seem unnecessary to urge its value upon even the stupidest of creatures. Yet it is a fact that the importance of thorough education of girls is still doubted—usually, of course, by men with deficient education of their own and an elaborate sense of their own importance and superiority.

Mary Lyon, whose noble efforts established Mount Holyoke College, and spread the idea of higher education for women throughout the world, put the case of women's education in a nutshell. She said:

"I think it less essential that the farmers and mechanics should be educated than that their wives, the mothers of their children, should be."

The education of a girl is important chiefly because it means the educating of a future mother. Whose brain but the mother's inspires and directs the son in the early years, when knowledge is most easily absorbed and permanently retained?

If you find in history a man whose success is based on intellectual equipment, you find almost invariably that his mother was exceptionally fortunate in her opportunities for education.

Well-educated women are essential to humanity. They insure abler men in the future, and incidentally they make the ignorant man feel ashamed of himself in the present.

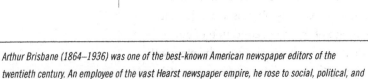

Arthur Brisbane (1864–1936) was one of the best-known American newspaper editors of the twentieth century. An employee of the vast Hearst newspaper empire, he rose to social, political, and financial influence that has never been equaled by another newspaper editor.

EXERCISE TWO:

Answer the following questions about Arthur Brisbane's editorial, "Why Women Should Vote." Be certain to base your answers on what the editorial actually says and not on your reaction—either positive or negative—to the editorial or the editor who wrote it.

1. How many theses does this editorial argue? What is it? / What are they?

They argue 2, women should vote and women deserve an education.

Beginning with the fourth paragraph, Brisbane makes 20 claims in support of his argument(s). Of these…

2. …approximately how many are facts?

about 6

Give one example:

3. ...approximately how many are interpretations of fact?

a few (8)

Give one example:

the 2nd to last paragraph

4. ...approximately how many are opinions?

a lot (7)

Give one example:

"I think it is less essential that the farmers & mechanics should be educated than that their wives..."

5. Approximately how many are presented as specific illustrations or evidence of the validity of his claim?

1

Give one example:

The blustering politician...

6. Does this editorial seem to be slanted toward an audience of a particular gender or age? What evidence suggests this?

   Yes, because it leans toward women and why they should fight for rights because they are calling men rude things

7. Does the information in this editorial seem to be spun to one view or conclusion over another? What evidence suggests this?

   yes, all the opinions in the editorial can show the amount it was spun.

   there are far too less facts to spin.

8. Is this editorial biased? What evidence suggests this?

   yes, it is biased towards women and how they should fight for rights.

   the lack of factual evidence - bias.

WHEN WILL WOMAN'S MENTAL LIFE BEGIN?
BY ARTHUR BRISBANE

It is pathetic to hear women of intelligence arguing in support of woman's claim to "equality" with man.

Of course, woman is really man's superior in important matters. She is vastly superior morally, beyond any question.

She does the greatest work in the world; she gives to earth its thinking population and creates every one of the great men that move civilization along.—

But otherwise, in the way of MATERIAL accomplishment, woman cannot be said to equal man at present, and she cannot be said ever to have equaled him.

Many of the most intelligent women demand recognition for woman as equal or superior to man in all ways.

They are deeply hurt if in gentle, patient reply you ask them to mention a female equivalent to a Newton, Archimedes or Shakespeare. It annoys them to tell them that a million autopsies prove fundamental differences between male and female brains in favor of the former—at least as regards volume and depth of cerebral convolutions.

Sometimes, after you have listened to a proud, high-spirited woman trying to prove that women would equal men in material accomplishment, if only they had a chance, you get so sad that you find yourself helping her out—digging up De Sevignes, De Staels, and other "great" women who have made up in brains for what they perhaps lacked in femininity.—

It is necessary to bear in mind that this earth, when man was turned loose upon it, was really a sort of desert island. It was a conglomeration of swamps, forests, deserts—all filled with wild beasts. Even the human beings, struggling feebly toward better days, were not far from the beasts at first. (They are not very far from them even now.)

Two kinds of work had to be done. The men had to fight, dig, hunt, drain marshes and murder each other.

The women had to SUPPLY THE MEN to do all the working and fighting and killing.

Beasts, wars, fevers killed off the sons of women almost as fast as they could bear them. Women must supply the demand for soldiers and workers and at the same time a surplus big enough to populate the globe. Thus far she has put on earth fourteen hundred millions of her own kind. Quite an achievement, we should say, when the career of a Napoleon or an Alexander called for a couple of million of men extra, or a plague like the black death, due to man's stupid lack of cleanliness, wiped out two-thirds of Europe's people.—

Men were the material workers—of course they exceeded in material achievement the women nursing babies at home.

But woman, caring for her children, sacrificing her life for them, developed on earth the moral sentiments, started each generation on its career a little better than its predecessor. She could not do all this and do the material things as well. In fact, she could not even THINK except on matters very near to her cradle, or her affections.

Remember that throughout the world's history it has been the lot of a vast majority of women to be constantly caring for young infants, or young children. Families of twenty children, or even more, have been common. It is probable that woman from the beginning of our racial existence until now has been the mother of from fifteen to twenty-five children on an average.

The dullest mind can see what that means.

Atrocious suffering. Endless worry about the children. Constant warfare against the man's selfish brutality.

How could woman rear her twenty children and at the same time do other work? How could she keep every thought, every effort of her brain on her offspring and develop her mind in other ways at the same time?

Give a man one young child to take care of FOR ONE DAY, and when you return to him you find a semi-imbecile, half-tearful creature.

In every great man's life you hear some remark of
this sort: "How can I work, Maria, if you let the
children make such a noise?"

Well, how could the millions of Marias work
with the children hanging to their skirts all
through history?—

But a better day is ahead for woman, and we are
proud to point it out to her.

Wise men begin to wonder what we shall do
when the earth is fully peopled? Shall we kill
surplus babies, or what shall we do?

There will be no surplus babies. Nature will
arrange that.

For every two human beings on earth two new
ones will be born.

Wars will be ended. Common sense will have
done away with the unnecessary illness which
now robs millions of mothers.

No woman will have more than two children.
Education will be understood. Women will not
be slaves to their babies. They will be admired
and thanked and made happy before the babies
arrive—instead of being half ashamed, as at
present.

The rearing of children will be simple. Each woman, instead of devoting twenty years of her life to child slavery, will have practically her whole life to devote to other things. She will be able to cultivate her mind. She will have more of a hold on Mr. Selfish Man, and he will have to pay more attention to her.

WOMAN'S hour of full mental development will arrive with the final and complete population of the globe, just as man's day of real mental growth will come after he shall have mastered the forces of nature and learned the elements of true social science.

. . .

Even then we do not anticipate that repulsive "equality" between men and women which is so much prated about.

The complete human being is not A MAN, nor is it A WOMAN. The COMPLETE human being is a man AND a woman. The TWO MAKE ONE. Each will contribute a share to the perfection of the whole. That was the way it was planned from the beginning, and we think we could prove it, if this column were six feet longer.

EXERCISE THREE

Answer the following questions about Arthur Brisbane's editorial, "When Will Woman's Mental Life Begin?" Be certain to base your answers on what the editorial actually says and not on your reaction—either positive or negative—to the editorial or the editor who wrote it.

1. What is Brisbane's thesis in this editorial?

"But otherwise, in the Way the MATERIAL accomplishment, woman cannot be said..."

2. What are some of the claims he makes in support of this thesis?

- The men had to do work, while the woman "supply the men"

- they populate the globe, and take care of children.

- men are material workers

- men cannot take care of children

3. What facts does Brisbane offer in support of these claims?

The fact about how the men are out and killing beasts and expanding land. Twenty to a family was common.

There are no facts

4. List and identify some notable propaganda techniques, logical fallacies, or rhetorical devices used in this editorial.

The wording, he uses emotion packed words.

name calling
self-evident truth
self begging truth

5. The editorial has an overall academic, objective tone. Is the editorial academic and objective or is there evidence of bias? If so, what evidence is there?

The editorial is extremey bias
lack of factual data

Writing Opportunity One: Write an essay in which you either support or refute the thesis of one of Brisbane's editorials. Be certain to support your own thesis with evidence from your own education and experience.

Chapter Four

INFORMATIVE AND ENTERTAINING NONFICTION

Most of the nonfiction you are likely to read, aside from dull school textbooks, will be informative pieces like news articles, entertaining pieces like personal and anecdotal entries in print or electronic journals, or feature articles that combine elements of both. Whether you're reading for information or enjoyment, however, and whether the writer's ultimate purpose is to teach or to entertain, the precepts of nonfiction remain the same.

Remember that all writers approach a topic from their personal viewpoints, so even an article intended solely to communicate facts about a little-known topic needs to be examined for the author's slant, attempts to spin the information in a particular direction, or outright bias. Not to do so is to read carelessly and to invite the possibility of being manipulated into accepting a questionable conclusion without question.

Consider the following selections: an essay by historian Bruce Catton and a travelogue by Tony Perrottet. Notice how, on the surface, they seem purely informative and reflective. On closer examination, however, it becomes clear that both authors have a point they hope their readers will at least consider, possibly in contrast to a previously held view.

By calling his essay "A Study..." Catton clearly establishes that this is going to be an informative piece. The reader need not look for a thesis or for evidence to support an argument.

GRANT AND LEE: A STUDY IN CONTRASTS
BY BRUCE CATTON

When Ulysses S. Grant and Robert E. Lee met in the parlor of a modest house at Appomattox Court House, Virginia, on April 9, 1865, to work out the terms for the surrender of Lee's Army of Northern Virginia, a great chapter on American life came to a close, and a great new chapter began.

These men were bringing the Civil War to its virtual finish. To be sure, other armies had yet to surrender, and for a few days the fugitive Confederate government would struggle desperately and vainly, trying to find some way to go on living now that its chief support was gone. But in effect it was all over when Grant and Lee signed the papers. And the little room where they wrote out the terns was the scene of one of the poignant, dramatic contrasts in American History.

Catton uses the word "contrasts" in his title and again here in his second paragraph. This is an informative, not a persuasive, piece so Catton heightens reader interest by emphasizing the magnitude and the importance of the contrast.

They were two strong men these oddly different generals, and they represented the strengths of two conflicting currents that through them, had come into final collision.

Back of Robert E. Lee was the notion that the old aristocratic concept might somehow survive and be dominant in American life.

Lee was tidewater Virginia, and in his

background were family, culture, and tradition
… the age of chivalry transplanted to a New
World which was making its own legends and its
own myths. He embodied a way of life that had
come down through the age of knighthood and
the English country squire. America was a land
that was beginning all over again, dedicated to
nothing much more complicated than the rather
hazy belief that all men had equal rights and
should have an equal chance in the world. In
such a land Lee stood for the feeling that it was
somehow of advantage to human society to have
a pronounced inequality in the social structure.
There should be a leisure class, backed by
ownership of land; in turn, society itself should
be tied to the land as the chief source of wealth
and influence. It would bring forth (according
to this ideal) a class of men with a strong sense
of obligation to the community; men who lived
not to gain advantage for themselves, but to meet
the solemn obligations which had been laid on
them by the very fact that they were privileged.
From them the country would get its leadership.
To them it could look for higher values—of
thought, of conduct, or personal deportment—to
give it strength and virtue.

> Within his overall discussion of Lee, Catton seems to be following a point-to-point comparison structure.

Lee embodied the noblest elements of this
aristocratic ideal. Through him, the landed
nobility justified itself. For four years, the
Southern states had fought a desperate war to
uphold the ideals for which Lee stood. In the
end, it almost seemed as if the Confederacy
fought for Lee; as if he himself was the
Confederacy … the best thing that the way of
life for which the Confederacy stood could ever
have to offer. He had passed into legend before
Appomattox. Thousands of tired, underfed,

> Catton here is expressing admiration for the man even as he suggests disapproval of the man's ideals.

> Here is the point at which Catton begins to transition from Lee the man to Lee the symbol of the South.

poorly clothed Confederate soldiers, long since past the simple enthusiasm of the early days of the struggle, somehow considered Lee the symbol of everything for which they had been willing to die. But they could not quite put this feeling into words. If the Lost Cause, sanctified by so much heroism and so many deaths, had a living justification, its justification was General Lee.

Grant, the son of a tanner on the Western frontier, was everything Lee was not. He had come up the hard way and embodied nothing in particular except the eternal toughness and sinewy fiber of the men who grew up beyond the mountains. He was one of a body of men who owed reverence and obeisance to no one, who were self-reliant to a fault, who cared hardly anything for the past but who had a sharp eye for the future.

Notice that, while Catton refers to Lee as an ideal, he speaks of Grant as a fully flesh-and-blood person.

These frontier men were the precise opposites of the tidewater aristocrats. Back of them, in the great surge that had taken people over the Alleghenies and into the opening Western country, there was a deep, implicit dissatisfaction with a past that had settled into grooves. They stood for democracy, not from any reasoned conclusion about the proper ordering of human society, but simply because they had grown up in the middle of democracy and knew how it worked. Their society might have privileges, but they would be privileges each man had won for himself. Forms and patterns meant nothing. No man was born to anything, except perhaps to a chance to show how far he could rise. Life was competition.

Yet along with this feeling had come a deep sense of belonging to a national community. The Westerner who developed a farm, opened a shop, or set up in business as a trader could hope to prosper only as his own community prospered—and his community ran from the Atlantic to the Pacific and from Canada down to Mexico. If the land was settled, with towns and highways and accessible markets, he could better himself. He saw his fate in terms of the nation's own destiny. As its horizons expanded, so did his. He had, in other words, an acute dollars-and-cents stake in the continued growth and development of his country.

> Notice that, according to Catton, both Lee and Grant represent some form of community.

And that, perhaps, is where the contrast between Grant and Lee becomes most striking. The Virginia aristocrat, inevitably, saw himself in relation to his own region. He lived in a static society which could endure almost anything except change. Instinctively, his first loyalty would go to the locality in which that society existed. He would fight to the limit of endurance to defend it, because in defending it he was defending everything that gave his own life its deepest meaning.

> Not an individual, not Lee, but the aristocrat—the archetype.

The Westerner, on the other hand, would fight with an equal tenacity for the broader concept of society. He fought so because everything he lived by was tied to growth, expansion, and a constantly widening horizon. What he lived by would survive or fall with the nation itself. He could not possibly stand by unmoved in the face of an attempt to destroy the Union. He would combat it with everything he had, because he could only see it as an effort to cut the ground out from under his feet.

> Not an individual, not Grant, but the Westerner—the archetype.

Note the metaphor.

Note the vivid imagery.

Just as each of the men came to stand as a metaphor for some aspect of American life, now they jointly come to represent the positive American traits both sides of the conflict shared.

So Grant and Lee were in complete contrast, representing two diametrically opposed elements in American life. Grant was the modern man emerging; beyond him, ready to come on the stage was the great age of steel and machinery, of crowded cities and a restless burgeoning vitality. Lee might have ridden down from the old age of chivalry, lance in hand, silken banner fluttering over his head. Each man was the perfect champion for his cause, drawing both his strengths and his weaknesses from the people he led.

Yet it was not all contrast, after all. Different as they were—in background, in personality, in underlying aspiration—these two great soldiers had much in common. Under everything else, they were marvelous fighters. Furthermore, their fighting qualities were really very much alike.

Each man had, to begin with, the great virtue of utter tenacity and fidelity. Grant fought his way down the Mississippi Valley in spite of acute personal discouragement and profound military handicaps. Lee hung on in the trench at Petersburg after hope born of a fighter's refusal to give up as long as he can still remain on his feet and lift his two fists.

Daring and resourcefulness they had, too: the ability to think faster and move faster than the enemy. These were the qualities which gave Lee the dazzling campaigns of Second Manassas and Chancellorsville and won Vicksburg for Grant.

Lastly, and perhaps greatest of all, there was the
ability, at the end, to turn quickly from the war
to peace once the fighting was over. Out of the
way these two men behaved at Appomattox
came the possibility of peace of reconciliation. It
was a possibility not wholly realized, in the years
to come, but which did, in the end, help the two
sections to become one nation again ... after a
war whose bitterness might have seemed to make
such a reunion wholly impossible. No part of
either man's life became him more than the part
he played in their brief meeting in the McLean
house at Appomattox. Their behavior there put
all succeeding generations of Americans in their
debt. Two great Americans, Grant and Lee—very
different, yet under everything very much alike.
Their encounter at Appomattox was one of the
great moments of American history.

Bruce Catton (1899-1978) was a Civil War specialist whose early career included reporting for various newspapers. In 1954, he received both the Pulitzer Prize for historical work and the National Book Award. He served as director of information for the United States Department of Commerce and wrote many books, including Mr. Lincoln's Army *(1951),* Glory Road *(1952),* A Stillness at Appomattox *(1953),* The Hallowed Ground *(1956),* America Goes to War *(1958),* The Coming Fury *(1961),* Terrible Swift Sword *(1963),* Never Call Retreat *(1966),* Waiting for the Morning Train: An American Boyhood *(1972), and* Gettysburg: The Final Fury *(1974). For five years, Catton edited* American Heritage *magazine.*

"Grant and Lee: A Study in Contrasts" was written as a chapter of The American Story, *1990.*

EXERCISE ONE:

Answer the following questions about Bruce Catton's "Grant and Lee: A Study in Contrasts."

1. What is implied by Catton's opening description of Lee as subscribing to "the notion that the old aristocratic concept might somehow survive and be dominant"?

OK

> Catton is saying that the way Lee does things are a little outdated, so if he was able to win like this, it would be amazing. shows slant toward grant.

2. What does Catton's use of the words "family, culture, and tradition" suggest?

3. What are some implicitly negative values that Catton associates with Lee?

−.5

> Catton associates an "old aristocratic concept...", he is saying that the way he does things and his values are outdated. inequality, paternalism

4. What are some implicitly positive values that Catton associates with Lee?

_____

_____

_____

_____

_____

5. What is implied by Catton's saying that Grant "was everything Lee was not"?

_____

_____

_____

_____

_____

6. Although Catton presents this essay as a comparison of Robert E. Lee and Ulysses S. Grant, these men ultimately become metaphors for what larger idea?

They become metaphors for the 2 views on america / the civil war. Lee represents the confederates, and Grant is the Union. 2 conflicting streams. → old   new

7. List some key words Catton uses to describe Grant's role as "the modern man emerging."

_____

_____

_____

_____

_____

_____

_____

8. What traits did Grant and Lee share that allow Catton to conclude that they were both "great Americans"?

They both are marvelous fighters as well as they both have venacity and fidelity. They are also daring & resourceful. Fasily they can change from war to peace.

9. What evidence of slant is there in this essay?

The slant is that the author is saying that both Lee & Grant are both amazing, so he/she will not offend either side. slant towards Grant. Lee = outdated ideals while ∨ = new →

10. Does Catton reveal any bias in this essay? What evidence can you provide to support your assertion?

_____

_____

_____

_____

_____

_____

DESTINATION AMERICA:
MOUNT RUSHMORE
BY TONY PERROTTET

With a Native American superintendent, the South Dakota monument is becoming much more than a shrine to four presidents.

The author begins immediately with an allusion to a classic film, thus already beginning to identify his audience.

Blame it on Cary Grant. The climactic chase in Hitchcock's 1959 thriller *North by Northwest*, in which he and Eva Marie Saint are pursued by foreign spies around the faces of George Washington, Abraham Lincoln, Thomas Jefferson and Theodore Roosevelt, is what fixed the idea in tourists' imaginations. Today the first question out of many visitors' mouths is not why, or even how, Mount Rushmore was carved, but can they climb it. Actually, it's not such a far-fetched question. Sculptor Gutzon Borglum's 1935 conception for the monument called for a grand public stairway leading from the base of the mountain to a hall of records, behind the presidential heads. But when the artist ran out of quality granite, and the project ran out of money, the plan was shelved. Climbing on the memorial has been officially prohibited since work ended there in 1941. In fact, even Hitchcock had to shoot his famous chase scene on a replica built in a Hollywood studio.

This is not an editorial, so we are not looking for a thesis. We are, however, looking for the slant—the author's reason for writing about this monument.

Which is why a special invitation from the park superintendent to "summit" Mount Rushmore is not something one can easily turn down. Early one morning, I and several other lucky hikers silently followed park ranger Darrin Oestmann on a trail through a sweetly scented ponderosa forest in the Black Hills of South Dakota, listening to birdsong and the cracking of twigs from passing goats. Scattered along the path were rusting nails, wires and lengths of air compression pipes, all left by the 400 or so local laborers who from 1927 to 1941 followed this very route, by wooden stairs, on their Promethean task.

Oestmann paused to point out a rarely glimpsed view of George Washington's profile, gleaming in the morning light. Mount Rushmore has not looked so good in more than six decades. This past summer, the four presidents were given a high-tech face-lift; they were blasted with 150-degree water under high pressure. Sixty-four years' worth of dirt and lichens fell from the memorial. "Now the faces are whiter and a lot shinier," said Oestmann, who helped clean "about three quarters of the first president. You see that dot in Washington's left eyelid?" He pointed to a broken drill bit stuck in the stone. "You could hardly see that before."

About ten minutes later, we scrambled up a few steep boulders and squeezed through pine branches, then passed beyond a high-security fence. Near-vertical metal steps took us into a granite crevice that runs behind the presidential heads—an oblong sliver, looking like the secret entrance to a pharaoh's tomb. This, we are told, is the Hall of Records, the vault Borglum envisioned. The hall was to be a repository for the Declaration of Independence and the U.S. Constitution. Worried that generations from now

Notice the vivid imagery. The feature article creates atmosphere—attempts to recreate the author's experience—as much as it communicates fact.

Another allusion. A "Promethean task" is one that is completed cleverly or creatively. Perrottet is not commenting on the magnitude or difficulty of the task; he is pointing out the artistry of it.

Notice the two similes, both comparing the Mount Rushmore monument to ancient archeological treasures. The author's point is subtle but clear. To him, Mount Rushmore is a valuable work, newer than, but comparable to, such wonders as the pyramids and Stonehenge.

The tone is sympathetic to both the artist and the monument.

Note the structural shift in the feature. The last paragraph was still telling us about Perrottet's experience. This paragraph begins to give us some factual background. If this were a short story, it would be part of the plot exposition.

The use of dashes and the insertion of a relatively irreverent reference to money help to create an informal, conversational, and mildly humorous tone.

people might find Mount Rushmore as enigmatic as Stonehenge, the sculptor also wanted to store information about the four presidents, as well as a record of American history and an explanation of, as he put it, "how the memorial was built and frankly, why."

The vault was never finished. Today, it's an ever-narrowing passage, honeycombed with drill marks, that stretches about 80 feet into the rock. Still, in 1998, Borglum's wish was partly fulfilled when the park service placed a teak box in a titanium cast in a hole they drilled at the hall's entrance. The box contained 16 porcelain panels covered with historical data, including a biography of the artist and his struggles to carve the memorial.

But the highpoint of the climb was yet to come. As Oestmann led us up the last steep stairway, we burst from the shadows into brilliant sunshine—on top of George Washington's head, 500 feet above the visitor center and 5,725 feet above sea level. As I wandered jelly-kneed over to Jefferson's and Lincoln's white pates— thankfully, their tops are relatively flat—the exhilarating view across the craggy, pine-covered Black Hills seemed never-ending.

Gutzon Borglum first stood on this spot in August 1925, when the memorial was still a half-formed dream. The idea for a titanic public sculpture came from South Dakota state historian Doane Robinson, who hoped it would lure more tourists—and their dollars—to the remote and impoverished state. The Black Hills, which boasted some of South Dakota's most spectacular scenery, were the obvious location, and in mid-1924 Robinson invited Borglum, one of America's leading sculptors, to create it. It was a fortuitous choice: he was an obsessive artist and consummate showman, by turns inspired, energetic, egotistical and abrasive, who despite his success (he was one of the first American sculptors to have work—two pieces—purchased by the Metropolitan Museum of Art in New York) still yearned for a project that would earn him immortality.

Dismissing Robinson's idea that the sculpture should feature Western heroes such as Lewis and Clark, Chief Red Cloud and Buffalo Bill, Borglum decided to carve the presidents, and he arrived in Rapid City with great fanfare that summer to search the rugged landscape for the optimal site. The cliff-face of Mount Rushmore seemed to offer the best granite and the best setting: a sunny, eastern exposure. In mid-August 1925, the sculptor, his 13-year-old son, Lincoln, and Robinson traveled with a local guide on horseback to the mountain to climb it to get a closer look. Standing on the summit, Borglum gazed out on the Black Hills and seemed—if only for a moment—humbled by the undertaking.

"I was conscious we were in another world...," Borglum later wrote. "And there a new thought seized me...the scale of that mountain peak.... It came over me in an almost terrifying manner that I had never sensed what I was planning." At age 58 the artist was contemplating a work nearly as ambitious as the ancient Colossus of Rhodes without any secure source of funding in a location unreachable by road. Its creation would be an epic battle, not only against nature, but against government agencies controlling the purse strings.

Yet another simile likening Mount Rushmore to a famous work of antiquity.

Oestmann calls our attention to red plotting points around Lincoln's eyes and green numbers along his hairline—revealed during preparation for the memorial's cleaning. He offers to take my photograph perched on Jefferson. "Don't go any farther back," he warns, as I maneuver cautiously into position.

The shift in grammatical mood indicated by the phrase "might seem" suggests a probable shift in the overall tone of the article.

Mount Rushmore might seem the most immutable of America's historical monuments. After all, what can possibly change on those stone faces, which seem to gaze down indifferently on the follies of their countrymen? Quite a lot, as it happens—including a seismic cultural shift traceable to the appointment, in 2004, of Gerard Baker, Mount Rushmore's first American Indian superintendent. Baker, 52, a Mandan-Hidatsa raised on the Fort Berthold Reservation in western North Dakota, has begun to expand programs and lectures at the monument to include the Indian perspective. Until recently, visitors learned about Rushmore as a patriotic symbol, as a work of art or as a geological formation, but nothing about its pre-white history—or why it raises such bitterness among many Native Americans.

Here Perrottet makes clear the exact nature of the article's shift in tone and focus.

Perrottet quotes Gerard Baker extensively to establish that he is portraying Gerard's view accurately, without slant or bias, in his interpretation of what Baker is saying.

"A lot of Indian people look at Mount Rushmore as a symbol of what white people did to this country when they arrived—took the land from the Indians and desecrated it," Baker says. "I'm not going to concentrate on that. But there is a huge need for Anglo-Americans to understand the Black Hills before the arrival of the white men. We need to talk about the first 150 years of America and what that means."

Indeed, Borglum erected his "shrine of democracy" on sanctified ground. *Paha Sapa*, meaning Black Hills in Lakota, were—and remain—a sacred landscape to many Indian nations, some of whom regard them as the center of the world. Natural formations such as Bear Butte and the Devil's Tower (over the border in Wyoming) are the setting for prayers, vision quests and healing ceremonies, while Wind Cave, a vast underground complex of limestone tunnels, is revered as the place where the Lakota emerged from the underworld to earth. Under the 1868 Treaty of Fort Laramie, Congress confirmed that the area would remain inviolate as the core of the Greater Sioux Reservation. But only six years later, in 1874, President Ulysses S. Grant ordered a military "reconnaissance" of the Black Hills, possibly because of rumors of gold in the mountains. He put the operation under the command of Lt. Col. George Armstrong Custer. In July 1874, Custer led a small army of more than 1,000 men, including cavalry and infantry, Indian scouts, interpreters, guides and civilian scientists, into the region with over 100 canvas wagons, 3 Gatling guns and a cannon.

Notice that this second "half" of the article is more factual and less narrative in style.

This formidable group behaved, in the words of author Evan S. Connell, "less like a military reconnaissance than a summer excursion through the Catskills." According to surviving letters and diaries, the men were bewitched by the Black Hills' beauty. These mountains, some of the oldest in North America, and their pine-filled valleys form a verdant oasis in the Great Plains. In the summer of 1874, crusty cavalrymen would lean from their horses to pluck bouquets

READING AND ANALYZING NONFICTION: SLANT, SPIN, AND BIAS

of wildflowers, and officers enjoyed champagne and wild gooseberries while the enlisted men played baseball. Custer expanded his natural history collection, loading a cart full of rare toads, petrified wood and rattlesnakes. "The air is serene and the sun is shining in all its glory," wrote Lt. James Calhoun, one of Custer's officers, in his diary. "The birds are singing sweetly, warbling their sweet notes as they soar aloft. Nature seems to smile on our movement."

But for the Lakota families who watched the group from the surrounding hilltops, the expedition foretold disaster. Custer's prospectors discovered gold in the mountains, and soon a rush to the Black Hills was on, with Deadwood, in the northern part of the region, one of the first illegal settlements. President Grant sent envoys to buy the Black Hills, but the Lakota refused to bargain: Lakota chief Sitting Bull said he would not sell so much as a pinch of dust. In the Great Sioux War that broke out in 1876 between the United States and a combined force of Lakota, Northern Cheyenne and Arapaho tribes, many of the cavalrymen who had plucked the Black Hills' flowers would lose their lives on the Little Bighorn in Montana—including Custer and Calhoun. The Lakota, however, were soon defeated, and, in 1877, Congress passed an act requiring them to relinquish their land and stay on reservations.

When Borglum arrived half a century later, the events leading up to the Indian Wars in the Black Hills were still fresh in many people's minds—Indians and whites. Yet few of Rushmore's planners seemed to have considered how the Native Americans might feel about the monument.

Several days following my tour of Rushmore, I visited the Defenders of the Black Hills, a Native American group that meets regularly in a Rapid City community center to inveigh against what they consider environmental affronts still scarring their lands, such as runoff from abandoned uranium mines, logging, drilling by mining companies, and the dumping of toxic waste. When I explained to the dozen men and women there—mostly Lakota, but also Ponca and Northern Cheyenne—that I was writing about the Mount Rushmore memorial, they laughed, then turned angry.

"Tell your readers that we'd like to blow it up!" said one.

"Cover those white faces up!"

"They call them the founding fathers? To us, they're the founding terrorists!"

Are these actual quotations? Probably. If Perrottet were to create them, or were to create them or take too much license condensing ideas into quotations, he would risk crossing the line into fiction.

The coordinator, a diminutive woman in her 50s named Charmaine White Face, a Lakota, spoke matter-of-factly. "We all hate Mount Rushmore," she said. "It's a sacred mountain that has been desecrated. It's like a slap in the face to us—salt in the wounds—as if a statue of Adolf Hitler was put up in the middle of Jerusalem."

Notice how this simile echoes Perrottet's comparisons of Mount Rushmore with ancient sacred locales like the pyramids and Stonehenge. The thrust of this simile is the polar opposite, however. The monument is not a sacred place; it is the desecration of a sacred place.

She handed me a badge: "The Black Hills Are Not For Sale," it read, referring to a 1980 court ruling that awarded the Sioux more than $100 million for the loss of the Hills. Though their communities remain desperately poor, the Lakota have refused the money, which has grown with interest to well over $500 million.

When I relay my encounter with the Defenders to Baker later, he smiles. "Hell, Indians are always telling me to blow up Mount Rushmore, but they know that's not going to happen." Sure, he says, the Black Hills were stolen from the Indians. "That's a historical fact. But we're not here at Mount Rushmore just to talk about broken treaties or make people feel guilty. The Defenders have a cause, and it's a good cause. But we're here at Mount Rushmore to educate."

These final paragraphs on Mount Rushmore are an attempt to reconcile the two opposing views Perrottet has presented.

Judy Olson, chief of interpretation at Mount Rushmore, says that there has been a strong positive response among Anglo visitors to new programs and exhibits that Baker has initiated, including a tepee manned by Lakota families. "We have four white guys up there. They represent the first century and a half of U.S. history. But there's a larger story to talk about. Who were the people here in the Black Hills before that? To broaden the old themes, to bring in other cultures, to include the good and the bad of American history, is what people want and need."

Crazy Horse Rides Again

"Fire in the hole! Fire in the hole! Fire in the hole!"

As the voice rings out, all eyes are fixed on a scarred mountainside where the enormous head and torso of the Lakota chief Crazy Horse can be clearly made out. He sits on horseback, his arm pointing toward the horizon. Then a dynamite blast tears the silence, sending a shower of granite boulders thundering to earth; the huge charge, one of two or three every week in summer, makes barely a dent in the neck of the warrior's horse.

Only 15 miles from Mount Rushmore, a monolithic new image is emerging from the Black Hills granite: a 563-foot-tall sculpture of the famous Native American who defeated Custer at Little Bighorn in 1876. Today a visit to the site testifies to the growing interest in Native American themes: even as a work in progress, Crazy Horse has already become a must-see counterpart to Mount Rushmore, luring more than one million visitors last year. (Rushmore had three million.)

Its scale is mind-boggling. When finished, the sculpture will be the world's largest mountain carving—dwarfing such monuments as the Great Pyramid of Giza and the Statue of Liberty. In fact, all four of Rushmore's presidents will fit inside Crazy Horse's 87.5-foot-tall head. The memorial depicts Crazy Horse responding to a taunt from a white trader before his death in 1877. Asked what had become of his lands, he replied: "My lands are where my dead lie buried."

The new monument was conceived in the late 1930s by Chief Henry Standing Bear, a Lakota. As Mount Rushmore neared completion, he wrote that he wanted to show the world that "the red man has great heroes, too." In 1939, the chief invited a muscular Boston sculptor, Korczak Ziolkowski, to undertake a sculpture of Crazy Horse. After serving in the Army in World War II, Ziolkowski leased a vast chunk of the Black Hills and started work on the monolith in 1948. "Every man has his mountain," he said at the time. "I'm carving mine!" In the late 1970s, looking like a latter-day Walt Whitman, with a huge white beard and a broad-rimmed hat, his wife and ten children laboring away at his side, he was still carving. Perhaps mindful of Borglum's years of wrangling with bureaucrats, Ziolkowski refused to let the U.S. government become involved in the project, twice turning down grants of $10 million. Instead, he funded the project with private donations and contributions from visitors. This meant that progress was slow. When Ziolkowski died in 1982, the sculpture was only a vague outline; many locals assumed it would be abandoned. But Ziolkowski's family rallied to continue the work. In 1998, Crazy Horse's completed face was unveiled, creating the sort of publicity that Borglum had enjoyed in 1930 when he revealed his first finished image, of Washington. Seemingly overnight, a chimerical project had become real, bringing streams of tourists intent upon learning more about Indian history. In 2000, a cathedral-like visitor center opened at the memorial, with a museum, Native American cultural center, and cinema. Plans also include a university and medical training center for Native Americans.

Notice the continuation of the sacred-locale theme.

When might the monolith be finished? "There's no way to estimate," says Ruth Ziolkowski, the sculptor's widow, who is nearly 80 and CEO and president of the nonprofit Crazy Horse Memorial Foundation. "It would be nothing but a wild guess anyway. We're not trying to be difficult. We just don't know. Korczak always said it wasn't important when it was finished as long as it was done right."

The carving is now overseen by Korczak's eldest son, Casimir, 52, who learned his skills on the rock-face with his father. "He was one of a kind, that's for sure," he says with a laugh. "We had our fights, like every father and son."

"Only in America could a man carve a mountain," Ziolkowski once declared—a sentiment that has not won over the Defenders of the Black Hills. They're not fans of this monument and say that it is as much of an environmental and spiritual violation of the Native lands as Borglum's work on Rushmore. Charmaine White Face, the Defenders' chairperson, says all work on Crazy Horse should cease at once: "Let nature reclaim the mountain!"

Tony Perrottet is an Australian-born writer living in the East Village of New York City. He is the author of Pagan Holiday, The Naked Olympics, *and most recently,* Napoleon's Privates *(Harper Collins); www. tonyperrottet.com.*

"Destination America: Mount Rushmore" first appeared in Smithsonian *magazine, May 2006, and is reprinted by permission of the author.*

EXERCISE TWO:

Answer the following questions about Tony Perrottet's "Destination America: Mount Rushmore."

1. What evidence does Perrottet provide to suggest that he values Mount Rushmore?

_____

_____

_____

_____

_____

_____

_____

2. In what ways is the feature article similar to a work of fiction, like a short story?

_____

_____

_____

_____

_____

_____

_____

3. In what ways is this feature article different from a work of fiction?

_____

_____

_____

_____

_____

_____

_____

_____

4. Perrottet makes it a point to comment on the sculptor's artistic arrogance.
   Does he seem to dislike Borglum? How do you know?

_____

_____

_____

_____

_____

_____

_____

_____

5. How does Perrottet signal to his reader that the tone and focus of his feature
   are going to change?

_____

_____

_____

_____

_____

_____

_____

_____

6. What facts about the interactions between the United States and Native
   American nations does Perrottet provide in this second half of his article?

   _____

   _____

   _____

   _____

   _____

   _____

   _____

7. What analysis of fact does he provide?

   _____

   _____

   _____

   _____

   _____

   _____

   _____

8. What interpretation of fact does he provide?

   _____

   _____

   _____

   _____

   _____

   _____

   _____

9. Is this portion of his article slanted or biased toward any particular view or audience? What evidence can you provide to support this?

_____

_____

_____

_____

_____

_____

10. What does Perrottet do to reconcile the United States and Native American views? How effective is the attempt? Does the attempt lessen any appearance of bias? Why or why not?

_____

_____

_____

_____

_____

_____

DECLARATION OF SENTIMENTS AND RESOLUTIONS
BY ELIZABETH CADY STANTON AND LUCRETIA MOTT

Declaration of Sentiments

Notice that the beginning of this declaration mirrors the opening of the Declaration of Independence of the United States.

When in the course of human events, it becomes necessary for one portion of the family of man to assume among the people of the earth a position different from that which they have hitherto occupied, but one to which the laws of nature and nature's God entitle them, a decent respect to the opinions of mankind requires that they should declare the causes that impel them to such a course.

Remember that the self-evident truth is a logical fallacy that denies the need for proof and allows for no alternative views.

We hold these truths to be self-evident: that all men and women are created equal; that they are endowed by their Creator with certain inalienable rights; that among these are life, liberty, and the pursuit of happiness; that to secure these rights governments are instituted, deriving their just powers from the consent of the governed. Whenever any form of government becomes destructive of these ends, it is the right of those who suffer from it to refuse allegiance to it, and to insist upon the institution of a new government, laying its foundation on such principles, and organizing its powers in such form, as to them shall seem most likely to effect their safety and happiness. Prudence, indeed, will dictate that governments long established should not be changed for light and transient

Notice key differences in wording between this declaration and the original.

causes; and accordingly all experience hath shown that mankind are more disposed to suffer while evils are sufferable, than to right themselves by abolishing the forms to which they accustomed. But when a long train of abuses and usurpations, pursuing invariably the same object, evinces a design to reduce them under absolute despotism, it is their duty to throw off such government, and to provide new guards for their future security. Such has been the patient sufferance of women under this government, and such is now the necessity which constrains them to demand the equal station to which they are entitled.

The history of mankind is a history of repeated injuries and usurpations on the part of man toward woman, having in direct object the establishment of an absolute tyranny over her. To prove this, let facts be submitted to a candid world.

- He has never permitted her to exercise her inalienable right to the elective franchise.

- He has compelled her to submit to laws, in the formation of which she had no voice.

- He has withheld from her rights which are given to the most ignorant and degraded men—both native and foreigner.

- Having deprived her of this first right of a citizen, the elective franchise, thereby leaving her without representation in the halls of legislation, he has oppressed her on all sides.

- He has made her, if married, in the eye of the law, civilly dead.

- He has taken from her all right in property, even to wages she earns.

- He has made her, morally, an irresponsible being, as she can commit many crimes with impunity, provided they can be done in the presence of her husband. In the covenant of marriage, she is compelled to promise obedience to her husband, he becoming, to all intents and purposes, her master—the law giving him power to deprive her of her liberty, and to administer chastisement.

- He has so framed the laws of divorce, as to what shall be the proper causes, and in case of separation, to who, the guardianship of the children shall be given, as to be wholly regardless of the happiness of women— the law, in all cases, going upon a false supposition of the supremacy of man, giving all power into his hands.

- After depriving her of all rights as a married woman, if single, and the owner of property, he has taxed her to support a government which recognizes her only when her property can be made profitable to it.

- He has monopolized nearly all the profitable employments, and from those she is permitted to follow, she receives but a scanty remuneration. He closes against her all the avenues to wealth and distinction which he considers most honorable to himself. As a teacher of theology, medicine, or law, she is not known.

- He has denied her the facilities for obtaining a thorough education, all colleges being closed against her.

- He allows her in Church, as well as State, but a subordinate position, claiming Apostolic authority for her exclusion from the ministry, and, with some exceptions, from any public participation in the affairs of the Church.

- He has created a false public sentiment by giving to the world a different code of morals for men and women, by which moral delinquencies which exclude women from society, are not only tolerated, but deemed of little account in man.

- He has usurped the prerogative of Jehovah himself, claiming it as his right to assign for her a sphere of action, when that belongs to her conscience and to her God.

- He has endeavored, in every way that he could, to destroy her confidence in her own powers, to lessen her self-respect and to make her willing to lead a dependent and abject life.

Now, in view of this entire disfranchisement of one-half the people of this country, their social and religious degradation—in view of the unjust laws above mentioned, and because women do feel themselves aggrieved, oppressed and fraudulently deprived of their most sacred rights, we insist that they have immediate admission to all the rights and privileges which belong to them as citizens of the United States.

In entering upon the great work before us, we anticipate no small amount of misconception, misrepresentation, and ridicule; but we shall use every instrumentality within our power to effect our object. We shall employ agents, circulate tracts, petition the State and National legislatures, and endeavor to enlist the pulpit and the press in our behalf. We hope this Convention will be followed by a series of Conventions embracing every part of the county.

Resolutions

Whereas, The great precept of nature is conceded to be, that "man shall pursue his own true and substantial happiness." Blackstone in his Commentaries remarks, that this law of Nature being coeval with mankind, and dictated by God himself, is of course superior in obligation to any other. It is binding over all the globe, in all countries and at all times; no human laws are of any validity if contrary to this, and such of them as are valid, derive their force, and all their validity, and all their authority mediately and immediately from this original; therefore,

Resolved, That all laws which prevent woman from occupying such a station in society as her conscience shall dictate, or which place her in a position inferior to that of man, are contrary to the great precept of nature, and therefore of no force or authority.

Resolved, That woman is man's equal—was intended to be so by the Creator, and the highest good of the race demands that she should be recognized as such.

Resolved, That the women of this country ought to be enlightened in regard to the laws under which they live, that they may no longer publish their degradation by declaring themselves satisfied with their present position, nor their ignorance, by asserting that they have all the rights they want.

Resolved, That inasmuch as man, while claiming for himself intellectual superiority, does accord to woman moral superiority, it is pre-eminently his duty to encourage her to speak and teach, as she has an opportunity, in all religious assemblies.

Resolved, That the same amount of virtue, delicacy, and refinement of behavior that is required of woman in the social state, should also be required of man, and the same transgressions should be visited with equal severity on both man and woman.

Resolved, That the objection of indelicacy and impropriety, which is so often brought against woman when she addresses a public audience, comes with a very ill-grace from those who encourage, by their attendance, her appearance on the stage, in the concert, or in feats of circus.

Resolved, That woman has too long rested satisfied in the circumscribed limits which corrupt customs and a perverted application of the Scriptures have marked out for her, and that it is time she should move in the enlarged sphere which her great Creator has assigned her.

Resolved, That it is the duty of women of this country to secure to themselves their sacred right to the elective franchise.

Resolved, That the equality of human rights results necessarily from the fact of the identity of the race in capabilities and responsibilities.

Resolved, That the speedy success of our cause depends upon the zealous and untiring efforts of both men and women, for the overthrow of the monopoly of the pulpit, and for the securing to women an equal participation with men in the various trades, professions, and commerce.

Resolved, therefore, That, being invested by the creator with the same capabilities, and the same consciousness of responsibility for their exercise, it is demonstrably the right and duty of woman, equally with man, to promote every righteous cause by every righteous means; and especially in regard to the great subjects of morals and religion, it is self-evidently her right to participate with her brother in teaching them, both in private and in public, by writing and by speaking, by any instrumentalities proper to be used, and in any assemblies proper to be held; and this being a self-evident truth growing out of the divinely implanted principles of human nature, any custom or authority adverse to it, whether modern or wearing the hoary sanction of antiquity, is to be regarded as a self-evident falsehood, and at war with mankind.

Anti-slave activist Lucretia Mott founded the Philadelphia Female Anti-Slavery Society in 1833 and led a delegation of women to the 1840 World Anti-Slavery Convention in London, where she was denied permission to speak because she was a woman. In 1848, she and fellow abolitionist Elizabeth Cady Stanton organized a Conference to Address Women's Rights and Issues in Seneca Falls, New York, at which the "Declaration of Sentiments and Resolutions" was drafted, adopted, and signed by sixty-eight women and thirty-two men.

EXERCISE THREE:

Answer the following questions about the "Declaration of Sentiments and Resolutions." Be certain to base your answers on what the editorial actually says and not on your reaction—either positive or negative—to the declaration itself or the persons who wrote it.

1. For what purpose might Stanton, Mott, and the others have chosen to begin their declaration with a series of logical fallacies?

_____

_____

_____

_____

_____

_____

2. To what extent are the facts presented verifiable facts, and to what extent are they unsupported claims and generalizations?

_____

_____

_____

_____

_____

_____

3. List any of the following logical fallacies and propaganda techniques that you find in this declaration.

Self-Evident Truth:

_____

_____

_____

_____

_____

_____

Begging the Question:

_____

_____

_____

_____

_____

_____

Unsupported Claims:

_____

_____

_____

_____

_____

Card-stacking:

_____

_____

_____

_____

_____

_____

Exaggerations:

_____

_____

_____

_____

_____

Appeals to Emotion:

_____

_____

_____

_____

_____

_____

Pinpointing the Enemy:

_____

_____

_____

_____

_____

_____

4. To what extent is this declaration a balanced argument in support of women's rights? To what extent is it propaganda?

_____

_____

_____

_____

_____

_____

Chapter Five

PERSUASIVE NONFICTION

The First Amendment to the Constitution of the United States guarantees Americans the rights to a free press and individual freedom of expression. Throughout the history of the United States, the American press has fought many times in the courts to protect both of these rights. Journalists have even been fined and imprisoned for their unwillingness to do something they saw as a potential threat to free speech and the free press.

One way the American press exercises its freedom and helps private citizens exercise their right is through the editorial page. In a printed newspaper, a section is usually dedicated to the expression of the opinions of the editorial staff of that newspaper. Many online journals, magazines, and newsletters also have editorial "pages" in which the editors of the site can express their views on current events.

Why should a newspaper's or e-journal's readers care to read the opinions of the journal's editors? Many don't, and many find themselves angered by the bias or the conservative (or the liberal) slant the editorials seem to take. Still, the presumption is that the editors—and the staffs of reporters who work for them—are closer to the news. They have followed the stories for days and weeks. They have eye-witnessed meetings and interviewed the subjects of their news stories. Many consider them to be in a better position to interpret facts and events, and many feel that the opinions of these editorial writers carry some weight.

Still, a careful reader must always remember that an editorial is, first and foremost, a statement of opinion. One expects a certain amount of slant, spin, or even bias in such a piece. The key is not to outright dismiss an argumentative piece simply because it argues a particular view (or to embrace it for the same reason); the key is to examine the selection for the presence of facts and interpretations and to make an educated and reasoned decision whether or not to agree with the editor's argument.

Consider the following three editorials from a series that ran in a newspaper in Oregon in 2005. The entire series of fifteen editorials, titled "Oregon's Forgotten Hospital," was awarded the 2006 Pulitzer Prize for Editorial Writing. Notice how the writers combine fact, interpretation, and opinion to illustrate and argue their point. Look to see where the writers have slanted their information or tone to appeal to a particular audience or spun their material to point to their conclusion.

Look to see, also, where the writers may have stacked the deck, begged the question, or used any of the other logical fallacies or techniques of propaganda that would begin to suggest bias.

Finally, compare the evidence you have looked for with what you have actually found, and make your own decision whether the writers' thesis is at all valid and whether they have presented a balanced argument in support of that thesis.

ALL THE LONELY PEOPLE
BY RICK ATTIG AND DOUG BATES

Eva York died in a bathtub in 1896 at the Oregon Asylum for the Insane. After an inquest, which absolved the hospital staff of any blame, no one claimed her corpse, so she was buried in the asylum cemetery and forgotten.

Eighteen years later Eva's remains were exhumed, cremated, placed in a copper urn and forgotten all over again. Today the corroding canister containing her ashes sits on a plain pine shelf in what's called the "Cremains Room" at the 122-year-old Salem institution, now known as the Oregon State Hospital.

> As all of these statements are verifiable, they count as facts. Notice that we do not yet know what the writers' thesis is.

Eva York is one of about 5,000 patients whose cremains are neatly stacked in that *stark, lonely room like cans of paint in a well-stocked hardware store.* Her story, one of the rare stories that can be told, thanks to the inquest into her death makes her a perfect symbol for what's wrong with the way Oregonians treat some of the most frail among us. The 2005 Legislature, which convenes Monday, must address this shameful truth.

> Whatever the room literally looks like, terms like "stark" and "lonely" and the simile render this statement the writers' interpretation.
>
> "Perfect symbol" is opinion.
>
> That there is something "wrong" and that the truth is "shameful" are opinions. This last sentence comes very close to revealing the writers' thesis.

The state hospital was a dumping ground in Eva's day, and to some extent it still is today. Even its administrators admit they're housing patients who don't belong there.

> "Dumping ground" is opinion. "Even its administrators" can be verified; therefore, it's a fact.

"Overcrowded" and "inadequate" are interpretations. "Warehoused" is an emotion-laden word, leaning towards propaganda.

Wards are overcrowded. Staffing is inadequate. Patients whose psychoses have been stabilized by medication are being warehoused in the hospital for lack of smaller community-based mental health centers that would be far better for them.

The grim, sprawling hospital is no place for juveniles, yet Oregon houses about a dozen frightened, troubled kids there. Some of the girls, often prior victims of sexual abuse, pull their mattresses out into hallways to sleep in safe view of staff. During the day, adolescents pass time outdoors in plain view, through concertina and barbed wire, of maximum-security adult patients.

These kids are left there, however, because Oregon has no proper facility for them. There's really nowhere else they can go.

Out of sight, out of mind. It's an age-old story of neglect for Oregon's most unfortunate. In fact, it was Eva York's story more than a century ago.

Today we know far more about Eva than any of her forgotten companions in the Cremains Room. That's because her death led to a story in Salem's Daily Capital Journal on Nov. 25, 1896.

Eva was a 36-year-old Marion County woman who probably wasn't even mentally ill. According to the old newspaper clipping, she was an epileptic, confined to the hospital's asylum-era epileptic ward five years before her death. In those days her malady, like depression and alcoholism, was viewed as akin to insanity.

Eva died between 2 and 3 p.m. on a Tuesday, "bath day" in the epileptic ward. While left unattended in a tub, she had a seizure and died from it, a coroner ruled. He found no evidence of drowning. An inquest jury declared the hospital to be "in no way responsible."

The news account went on to say the hospital telegraphed word of Eva's death to "a brother residing near Hubbard." Her remains, however, were never claimed.

All of this is verifiable, so it counts as fact. The fact that the writers provide a single example, however, should be considered from two viewpoints: the need not to make the editorial too long and the need to show that this one case is not the only case.

The entire asylum cemetery was exhumed in 1913-14 when the state decided it needed the land. Many of the headstones were unceremoniously dumped on a nearby hilltop. All unclaimed remains, including Eva's, were cremated and stored in a basement.

By 1976 that bleak collection of urns exceeded 5,000. That year, in a long overdue act of respect, they were placed underground in a modest memorial on the hospital grounds. But water seeped into the vaults, damaging the copper containers and destroying most of their paper labels. A few years ago, the cash-strapped institution unearthed the urns and stashed them in the Cremains Room, next to the incinerator where all the patients had been cremated.

If Eva York is a symbol of Oregon neglect, the hospital itself its physical hulk is a full-blown metaphor. The tub that she died in is still there, gathering mold and rat droppings in an abandoned wing that's creepier than any haunted house one might imagine.

The writers might be begging the question here if they assume their reader agrees that Eva York is a symbol.

Occupied spaces of the hospital are cheerier only by comparison. They comprise a foreboding, ramshackle collection of additions to the original 1883 structure along with several decrepit satellite buildings, the newest of which is more than a half-century old.

Patients spend their hours locked in jam-packed day rooms connected by long, dreary corridors to their prisonlike sleeping quarters, crammed with more bodies than they were designed for. They gaze out windows covered with oppressive security screens, and they stare at visitors coming and going on balky, creaky old elevators. No wonder the makers of "One Flew Over the Cuckoo's Nest," the Oscar-winning movie based on Ken Kesey's novel, chose to film it at the Oregon State Hospital. It was a fright 30 years ago, and the place still looks the same today.

Unlike the cinematic "Cuckoo's Nest" villains, however, the administrators and staff at today's Oregon State Hospital aren't the bad guys. They're pretty much doing the best they can with deplorable resources provided by a state with a long history of giving short shrift to its mentally ill.

Those running the institution, in fact, say they want change. They also voice support for a fledgling movement in the Legislature to create that change.

One man Senate President Peter Courtney, D-Salem lit the flame. Fed up with the state pouring money and crowding patients into the hospital, he engineered a $467,000 emergency appropriation last month to start a process that ought to lead to replacement of Oregon's disgraceful relic.

"Prisonlike" is both an interpretation and possibly an appeal to emotion.

That emergency money will pay for stopgap measures to relieve overcrowding. It also will launch work on a master plan that will give lawmakers a blueprint for a new, more humane way of caring for these patients.

On Monday, when the 2005 Oregon Legislature convenes, all 90 members should mark May 16 on their desk calendars. That's the deadline for presentation of this blueprint. It will likely call for a years-long project requiring tens of millions of dollars to build a smaller, modern hospital and an enlarged network of community mental health centers that would be less costly to operate and more effective at treating patients.

Every legislator must commit right now to moving Oregon mental health care out of the dark shadows of its 19th-century roots. And while they're at it, they should spend some money on a suitably dignified memorial for the earthly remains of Eva York and her fellow lost souls in the Cremains Room.

While the thesis has been implied since the end of the third paragraph, here is the first time it is actually articulated.

"All the Lonely People" is the first in an series of editorials and was originally published in The Oregonian on January 5, 2005. The entire series of fifteen editorials, titled "Oregon's Forgotten Hospital," was awarded the 2006 Pulitzer Prize for Editorial Writing.

EXERCISE ONE:

Answer the following questions about the editorial, "All the Lonely People." Be certain to base your answers on what the editorial actually says and not on your reaction—either positive or negative—to the editorial or the editors who wrote it.

1. List three facts, not already pointed out, that the writers include in their editorial.

_____

_____

_____

_____

_____

_____

_____

_____

2. List some statements that are clearly interpretations of fact. Highlight the words that show the statement to be an interpretation.

_____

_____

_____

_____

_____

_____

_____

_____

3. What might be the facts on which the interpretations you have identified are based?

_____

_____

_____

_____

_____

4. What facts might the writers have chosen to exclude from their description of conditions in the hospital?

_____

_____

_____

_____

_____

5. What are the two most likely reasons the writers chose not to include such facts?

_____

_____

_____

_____

_____

ONE FLEW OUT OF THE CUCKOO'S NEST
BY RICK ATTIG AND DOUG BATES

Cora Burnell says she remembers looking out a window at the Oregon State Hospital and seeing Jack Nicholson during the filming of "One Flew Over the Cuckoo's Nest" in 1975.

"In the movie, he was the crazy one. He got part of his brain taken out," Burnell says. "The big Indian, he was the strong one. And the nurse what was her name? she scared me."

Burnell's memory sometimes plays cruel tricks on her. She wasn't really there during the filming. She was 13 then and had just been diagnosed with schizoaffective disorder. But she's seen "Cuckoo's Nest" and has an intimate knowledge of the 122-year-old hospital where the movie was shot. She was locked up there for 12 years in a ward she describes as "a terrible place real creepy, but not as bad as in the movie."

Today, at 43, Burnell can attest to the need for tearing down the oppressive relic where the movie was made and replacing it with a smaller modern hospital and an expanded network of community-based treatment homes.

Burnell lives today in an ideal such place. She's one of five residents of Homestreet, a lovely old two-story house with a big wraparound porch in Hillsboro. The nonprofit treatment facility is a model of what modern mental health care ought to look like.

Yet hundreds of patients such as Burnell have been forced to remain too long in the dreary hospital, despite mounting evidence that long-term institutionalization does the mentally ill more harm than good. The problem: For too many years Oregon has failed to keep up with the national trend to community-based services while clinging to its aging "cuckoo's nest."

Burnell was 21 when she was sent there after stabbing a man in Portland during an episode of psychosis and substance abuse. She credits the hospital with stabilizing her disorder but thinks she made little progress during her long stay in the forensics ward.

"There was no Nurse Ratched," she says. "The nurses were real nice. So were the doctors. But the staff was not helpful. I think they were overworked."

She remembers the ward as much too crowded, "not clean enough" and utterly lacking in privacy. She never felt completely safe during her 12-year tenure or subsequent rehospitalizations.

Burnell feels just the opposite about her new life at Homestreet. Its staff of four goes far beyond just making sure the residents take their "meds." She and her housemates receive treatment at a level they could never dream of getting at the Salem institution.

Burnell, for example, has learned how to cook French toast and Italian pasta. She is receiving lessons in grocery shopping, personal hygiene, housekeeping, money management and coping skills. She has been shown how to catch the nearby MAX train for trips to Beaverton and Portland.

Within two years, Burnell is expected to make the transition to more independent living. On her bedroom wall at Homestreet, she says, hangs a picture of that dream "a beautiful, beautiful home" where she can live on her own. The picture shows a bright, cheerful apartment, she says, with privacy and plenty of space for Cinnamon Bear and the rest of her prized stuffed animals.

Homestreet and other forms of community-based treatment are not just more beneficial for most patients. They also are more cost-effective. The average monthly cost for a patient at the state hospital is $11,000, all of it out of Oregon's general fund with no federal match. Medicaid won't pay for patient care in state mental hospitals. But a month for Burnell at Homestreet costs the state only $3,375, and Medicaid picks up 62 percent of that.

To their credit, Oregon mental health officials are working hard to add community beds. But they also acknowledge that the Salem hospital still holds scores of patients who have been cleared for group-home treatment but have nowhere to go. The 2005 Legislature must get moving to help provide these resources.

Until then, it's to Oregon's shame that these patients remain warehoused in a decrepit institution. They are today's version of the forgotten patients whose canisters of unclaimed ashes are still stacked on shelves with no proper memorial in the hospital's grim "Cremains Room," where the standing photo for this series was taken.

On Monday, Oregon legislators will have a novel opportunity to experience something akin to what Burnell endures if her illness isn't under control. The National Alliance for the Mentally Ill is setting up a "virtual hallucination machine" in the Capitol to help lawmakers grasp the severe effects of schizophrenia and other such disorders.

Legislators should come away committed to support Senate Bill 222, which would broaden the range of community housing options for people such as Cora Burnell. And if the simulated hallucinations don't sway them, the lawmakers should visit her at Homestreet and see firsthand what ought to be the vision of mental health care in Oregon.

They won't actually find a picture on her wall showing the "beautiful, beautiful home" she talks about. It's only in her mind. But it's a picture that a humane Oregon should make real for all of the state's most vulnerable citizens.

"One Flew Out of the Cuckoo's Nest" is the second editorial in the Pulitzer Prize-winning series, "Oregon's Forgotten Hospital." It was originally published in The Oregonian *on January 30, 2005.*

EXERCISE TWO:

Answer the following questions about the editorial, "One Flew Out of the Cuckoo's Nest." Be certain to base your answers on what the editorial actually says and not on your reaction—either positive or negative—to the editorial or the editors who wrote it.

1. What is the editors' thesis in this editorial? At what point does this thesis become clear?

_____

_____

_____

_____

_____

_____

_____

2. List three facts that the writers include in their editorial.

_____

_____

_____

_____

_____

_____

3. List some statements that are clearly interpretations of fact. Highlight the words that show the statement to be an interpretation.

_____

_____

_____

_____

_____

_____

_____

4. What might be the facts on which the interpretations you have identified are based?

_____

_____

_____

_____

_____

_____

_____

5. List 3 or 4 value-laden words chosen by the writers to strengthen their argument.

_____

_____

_____

_____

_____

_____

_____

6. List and identify 3 or 4 other propaganda techniques or logical fallacies used by the writers to support their argument.

_____

_____

_____

_____

_____

_____

_____

7. Overall, is this editorial a balanced argument, or is it too slanted or biased in one direction? Why?

_____

_____

_____

_____

_____

_____

_____

A MAD AND MINDLESS
HEALTH POLICY
BY RICK ATTIG AND DOUG BATES

Kris Anderson, a single mom in Salem, opens
her mail and discovers another rejection notice
from her insurance company. She slumps to her
knees, then looks up to see her 9-year-old son,
who suffers from bipolar disorder, charging at
her with a hammer.

A slight, 14-year-old Portland boy, Jake Steckly,
sits in a Capitol hearing room and bravely tells
lawmakers how his brother's mental illness and
his father's substance abuse wiped out his family
financially, destroyed his parents' marriage and
made him want to run away. When the boy
begins to sob while describing visiting his dad in
a drug treatment program his mom paid for with
her credit card, tears trickle down the faces of
legislators.

The pain, unfairness and even the danger of
Oregon's discriminatory insurance system is plain
to see. Yet many Oregon leaders keep looking the
other way. Even when Boyd Owens, a suicidal
man with a 10-inch-long knife, forced his way
onto the Senate floor, coincidentally choosing
the same day mental health advocates had come
to the Capitol for "Mental Health Day," all the
nervous chatter among lawmakers afterward was
about increased security.

Security for them, of course. But not for the tens of thousands of Oregon families struggling with severe mental illnesses such as schizophrenia, bipolar disorder and clinical depression.

Oregon is one of the few states that still do not require mental-health parity in insurance. Thirty-five other states already have some form of a law preventing insurers from putting more restrictions, such as spending caps and hospitalization limits, on treatment of mental illness than for physical ailments. Neighboring Washington is preparing to pass a parity law; its House recently approved a parity bill by an overwhelming 67-25 vote.

There is a distant but real connection between this lack of insurance parity and the crisis at the Oregon State Hospital, a decrepit facility overflowing with patients. Oregon has a mental-health system that shifts the bulk of the costs to taxpayers, and all but invites its residents to get worse, to suffer more, to grow more desperate and dangerous, before they can get care.

Oregon has an insurance system that forces a mother like Anderson to beg and beg and beg for benefits for her troubled son. Even after her son was granted another 10 hours of care, and she and her doctor agreed to string it out with hurried, 10-minute visits, another letter soon arrived, explaining that Anderson was now, once and for all, out of benefits. She had missed the fine print, which read 10 hours, or 10 doctor visits, whichever came first.

Oregon's system is both cruel and discriminatory. Insurers do not tell a patient with a kidney disease that they will pay for 10 trips to the hospital for dialysis, but no more, ever. Yet when voices began to thunder inside the head of Kathy Larrabee's teenage son, and she took him to a Portland hospital where he was diagnosed with paranoid schizophrenia, she discovered her son was entitled to 10 days of inpatient treatment over his entire lifetime.

The 17-year-old boy came home from the hospital after two weeks, but promptly tried to commit suicide and was rehospitalized. Today, five years later, Larrabee's son is doing well on medication and enrolled at Portland State University, but Larrabee and her husband are still paying off tens of thousands of dollars in medical charges, even after selling a business and their former home overlooking Newport's bayfront.

Oregon has an insurance system that provided Jake Steckly's dad such a scant lifetime benefit for drug abuse treatment that it was exhausted before Jake was even born. This state still pretends that people with addictions, depression or even schizophrenia can be declared cured when the insurance coverage runs out in a few days.

To their credit, many Oregon leaders recognize the damage caused by this state's unfair health policy. Senate President Peter Courtney has given his parity bill the title of Senate Bill 1, and says, "There's no more important bill to me." Gov. Ted Kulongoski, whose task force on mental illness listed parity as its No. 1 legislative priority, supports the legislation.

Yet the insurance industry and powerful business groups, including Associated Oregon Industries, oppose mental health parity. So do Republican leaders in the Oregon House.

Parity foes say they fear an insurance mandate would increase costs and prompt some employers to stop offering health benefits entirely. That is a reasonable concern, but it's not borne out in the actual experience of states that have required parity for years.

Oregon also now has some of its own experience with parity: In 2003, the Oregon Public Employees' Benefit Board acquired mental-health parity for state employees including members of the Legislature and their dependents. In the first year, premium costs increased by less than one-half of 1 percent.

Meanwhile, denying mental health care doesn't lead to savings, it leads to more illness, absenteeism, crime, homelessness and poverty. Several studies cited by the National Mental Health Association show that costs of untreated mental illnesses to businesses, government and families nationally exceed $110 billion a year.

Oregon is not better off depriving the mentally ill of care, or pushing families into bankruptcy and onto public assistance. One of the cruelest effects of the state's current policy is that some parents are forced to give the state custody of their mentally ill children in order to get them care. That is one of Kris Anderson's worst fears. "My story isn't that bad yet," she says. "But my son is young, and we've exhausted most of the benefits available to him. I know what might lie ahead for us."

It should never come to that. Oregonians with mental illness should be cared for with the same urgency and compassion as those with physical ailments.

Jake Steckly remembers legislators wiping tears from their eyes, and standing and applauding his testimony. They were moved but only so far. That was 18 months ago, and a parity bill still has not yet come to a floor vote in either the Oregon House or Senate.

Steckly is 15 now, a sophomore at Lincoln High School. He's willing to go to Salem to testify again, if it would help. But this boy who's been through so much already has a fair question: "What else are they waiting to hear?"

"A Mad and Mindless Health Policy" is the third editorial in the Pulitzer Prize-winning series, "Oregon's Forgotten Hospital." It was originally published in The Oregonian *on February 13, 2005.*

Writing Opportunity One: Write an essay in which you evaluate this editorial as either a balanced argument or too slanted or biased in one direction. Be certain to base your evaluation on an analysis of the information and the approach of the editorial itself and not simply on the basis of whether you agree or disagree with the thesis.

Not all persuasive pieces are editorials or letters to the editor. Some are simply essays or reflections, commentaries from columnists in magazines, newspapers, webzines, and blogs. Some are speeches, intended to sway public opinion and motivate a group to perform an action. Still, however, the reader or audience must be sensitive to the writer's use of those elements that would indicate a particular slant or spin or suggest outright bias.

To allow oneself to be persuaded to a particular point of view or course of action by means of reason is one thing, but to allow oneself to be manipulated into agreeing on purely emotional grounds is potentially dangerous.

Consider the following essays, speeches, and declarations and examine the techniques used to sway the readers and listeners.

ON WOMEN'S RIGHT TO VOTE
BY SUSAN B. ANTHONY

Friends and fellow citizens, I stand before you tonight under indictment for the alleged crime of having voted at the last presidential election, without having a lawful right to vote. It shall be my work this evening to prove to you that in thus voting, I not only committed no crime, but, instead, simply exercised my citizen's rights, guaranteed to me and all United States citizens by the National Constitution, beyond the power of any state to deny.

Since the language of the Fourteenth Amendment (1868) does not specifically exclude women from its definition of "citizen" and protects the rights of all "citizens," Anthony turned out to vote in the 1872 presidential election. Two weeks after voting, she was arrested. At trial, she delivered this speech as part of her defense.

The preamble of the Federal Constitution says:

"We, the people of the United States, in order to form a more perfect union, establish justice, insure domestic tranquility, provide for the common defense, promote the general welfare, and secure the blessings of liberty to ourselves and our posterity, do ordain and establish this Constitution for the United States of America."

Absolutely aware of her audience and purpose—Anthony is defending herself in a court of law—she appeals immediately to the supreme law of the nation.

It was we, the people; not we, the white male citizens; nor yet we, the male citizens; but we, the whole people, who formed the Union. And we formed it, not to give the blessings of liberty, but to secure them; not to the half of ourselves and the half of our posterity, but to the whole people—women as well as men. And it is a downright mockery to talk to women of their enjoyment of the blessings of liberty while they are denied the use of the only means of securing them provided by this democratic-republican government—the ballot.

For any state to make sex a qualification that must ever result in the disfranchisement of one entire half of the people, is to pass a bill of attainder, or, an ex post facto law, and is therefore a violation of the supreme law of the land. By it the blessings of liberty are forever withheld from women and their female posterity. To them this government has no just powers derived from the consent of the governed. To them this government is not a democracy. It is not a republic. It is an odious aristocracy; a hateful oligarchy of sex; the most hateful aristocracy ever established on the face of the globe; an oligarchy of wealth, where the rich govern the poor. An oligarchy of learning, where the educated govern the ignorant, or even an oligarchy of race, where the Saxon rules the African, might be endured; but this oligarchy of sex, which makes father, brothers, husband, sons, the oligarchs over the mother and sisters, the wife and daughters, of every household— which ordains all men sovereigns, all women subjects, carries dissension, discord, and rebellion into every home of the nation.

Webster, Worcester, and Bouvier all define a citizen to be a person in the United States, entitled to vote and hold office.

Although Anthony does not cite the fact, these words are a direct quotation from the Declaration of Independence.

The only question left to be settled now is: Are women persons? And I hardly believe any of our opponents will have the hardihood to say they are not. Being persons, then, women are citizens; and no state has a right to make any law, or to enforce any old law, that shall abridge their privileges or immunities. Hence, every discrimination against women in the constitutions and laws of the several states is today null and void, precisely as is every one against Negroes.

This is a very carefully structured speech: first, a general appeal to the law's promise to protect the rights of all citizens; second, establishing the definition of "citizens" as "persons"; and third, the logical argument that, as women are persons, so they are citizens, and their rights are thereby protected by the law.

"On Women's Right to Vote" was delivered before the United States Circuit Court for the Northern District of New York at Canandaigua on June 19, 1873. Anthony was subsequently found guilty and fined $100 plus the cost of prosecution. The fine was never paid.

EXERCISE THREE:

Answer the following questions about the speech, "On Women's Right to Vote."
Be certain to base your answers on what the speech actually says and not on your
reaction—either positive or negative—to the topic or the writer.

1. What facts does Anthony use in support of her claim?

_____

_____

_____

_____

_____

_____

_____

_____

2. Which statements are interpretations of fact?

_____

_____

_____

_____

_____

_____

_____

_____

3. Which statements are statements of opinion?

_____

_____

_____

_____

_____

_____

_____

4. How persuasive is Anthony's speech? Why?

_____

_____

_____

_____

_____

_____

_____

_____

_____

BATTLE OF THE BABIES
BY AGNES REPPLIER

A warfare has been raging in our midst, the echoes of which have hardly yet died sullenly away upon either side of the Atlantic. It has been a bloodless and un-Homeric strife, not without humorous side-issues, as when Pistol and Bardolph and Fluellen come to cheer our anxious spirits at the siege of Harfleur[1]. Its first guns were heard in New York, where a modest periodical, devoted to the training of parents, opened fire upon those time-honored nursery legends which are presumably dear to the hearts of all rightly constituted babies. The leader of this gallant foray protested vehemently against all fairy tales of a mournful or sanguinary[2] cast, and her denunciation necessarily included many stories which have for generations been familiar to every little child. She rejected Red Riding Hood, because her own infancy was haunted and embittered by the evil behavior of the wolf; she would have none of Bluebeard, because he was a wholesale fiend and murderer; she would not even allow the pretty Babes in the Wood, because they tell a tale of cold-hearted cruelty and of helpless suffering; while all fierce narratives of giants and ogres and magicians were to be banished ruthlessly from our shelves. Verily, reading will be but gentle sport in the virtuous days to come.

An allusion to the Greek epics *The Iliad* and *The Odyssey*, both of which contain episodes of violence and bloodshed.

Don't miss Repplier's sarcasm.

---

1 *Pistol, Bardolph, and Fluellen are relatively comic characters in several of William Shakespeare's plays, most notably* Henry V. *Henry's siege of Harfleur is the focus of the play.*

2 *Violent and bloody.*

Now it chanced that this serious protest against nursery lore fell into the hands of Mr. Andrew Lang[1], the most light-hearted and conservative of critics, and partial withal to tales of bloodshed and adventure. How could it be otherwise with one reared on the bleak border land, and familiar from infancy with the wild border legends that Sir Walter knew and loved; with stories of Thomas the Rhymer, and the plundering Hardens, and the black witches of Loch Awe! It was natural that with the echoes of the old savage strife ringing in his ears, and with the memories of the dour Scottish bogies and warlocks lingering in his heart, Mr. Lang could but indifferently sympathize with those anxious parents who think the stories of Bluebeard and Jack the Giant Killer too shocking for infant ears to hear. Our grandmothers, he declared, were not ferocious old ladies, yet they told us these tales, and many more which were none the worse for hearing. "Not to know them is to be sadly ignorant, and to miss that which all people have relished in all ages." Moreover, it is apparent to him, and indeed to most of us, that we cannot take even our earliest steps in the world of literature, or in the shaded paths of knowledge, without encountering suffering and sin in some shape; while, as we advance a little further, these grisly forms fly ever on before. "Cain," remarks Mr. Lang, "killed Abel. The flood drowned quite a number of persons. David was not a stainless knight, and Henry VIII was nearly as bad as Bluebeard. Several deserving gentlemen were killed at Marathon. Front de Boeuf came to

---

1 Andrew Lang (1844–1912) was a Scottish man of letters. He is best known for his publication of a twelve-book series of collections of fairy tales, including "Little Red Riding Hood," "The Sleeping Beauty in the Wood," "Cinderella," and "Rapunzel."

an end shocking to sensibility, and to Mr. Ruskin."
*The Arabian Nights, Pilgrim's Progress, Paul and
Virginia*[1]—all the dear old nursery favorites must,
under the new dispensation, be banished from
our midst; and the rising generation of prigs must
be nourished exclusively on *Little Lord Fauntleroy*[2],
and other carefully selected specimens of milk-
and-water diet.

The prospect hardly seems inviting; but as the
English guns rattled merrily away in behalf of
English tradition, they were promptly met by
an answering roar from this side of the water.
A Boston paper rushed gallantly to the defense
of the New York periodical, and gave Mr.
Lang—to use a pet expression of his own—"his
kail through the reek." American children, it
appears, are too sensitively organized to endure
the unredeemed ferocity of the old fairy stories.
The British child may sleep soundly in its little
cot after hearing about the Babes in the Wood;
the American infant is prematurely saddened
by such unmerited misfortune. "If a consensus
of American mothers could be taken," says
the Boston writer, "our English critic might
be infinitely disgusted to know in how many
nurseries these cruel tales must be changed,
or not told at all to the children of less savage
generations. No mother nowadays tells them in
their unmitigated brutality."

Is this true, I wonder, and are our supersensitive
babies reared perforce on the optimistic version

---

1   *A French novel, originally published in 1787, that tells the
    tale of two childhood friends who fall in love and then are
    tragically killed in a shipwreck.*

2   *The first novel of Frances Hodgson Burnett, most famous for* A
    Little Princess *and* The Secret Garden.

of Red Riding Hood, where the wolf is cut open by the woodman, and the little girl and her grandmother jump out, safe and sound? Their New England champion speaks of the "intolerable misery"—a very strong phrase—which he suffered in infancy from having his nurse tell him of the Babes in the Wood; while the Scriptural stories were apparently every whit as unbearable and heart-breaking. "I remember," he says, "two children, strong, brave man and woman now, who in righteous rage plucked the Slaughter of the Innocents out from the family Bible." This was a radical measure, to say the least, and if many little boys and girls started in to expurgate the Scriptures in such liberal fashion, the holy book would soon present a sadly mutilated appearance.

Moreover, it seems to me that such an anecdote, narrated with admirable assurance, reveals very painfully the lack of a fine and delicate spirituality in the religious training of children; of that grace and distinction which are akin to saintship, and are united so charmingly in those to whom truth has been inseparably associated with beauty. There is a painting by Ghirlandaio hanging over the altar in the chapel of the Foundling Asylum in Florence. It represents the Adoration of the Magi, and kneeling by the side of the Wise Men is a little group of the Holy Innocents, their tiny garments stained with blood[1], their hands clasped in prayer; while the Divine Child turns from his mother's embraces, and from the kings' rich gifts to greet the little

Repplier's acknowledgment that this is her opinion helps to disarm charges of bias.

1 This is a reference to the episode in the second chapter of the Gospel of Matthew, in which an angry King Herod orders all boys in Judea two years old and under to be slain. His hope is to kill the infant Jesus.

companions who have yielded up their spotless lives for him. Now, surely those lean, brown Florentine orphans, who have always before their eyes this beautiful and tender picture, absorb through it alone a religious sentiment unfelt by American children who are familiar only with the ugly and inane prints of American Sunday-schools, in which I have known the line, "My soul doth magnify the Lord," to be illustrated by a man with a magnifying-glass in his hand. Possibly our Sunday-school scholars, being more accurately instructed as to dates, could inform the little Florentines that the Innocents were not slaughtered until after the Magi had returned to the East. But no child who had looked day after day upon Ghirlandaio's lovely picture—more appealing in its pathos than Holman Hunt's brilliant and jocund *Triumph of the Innocents*[1]— could desire to pluck "in righteous rage" that chapter from the Bible. He would have at least some dim and imperfect conception of the spiritual meaning, the spiritual joy, which underlie the pain and horror of the story.

This reflection will help us in some measure to come to a decision, when we return to the vexed problem of nursery tales and legends. I believe it is as well to cultivate a child's emotions as to cultivate his manners or his morals, and the first step in such a direction is necessarily taken through the stories told him in infancy. If a consensus of mothers would reject the good old fairy tales "in their unmitigated brutality," a consensus of men of letters would render a different verdict; and such men, who have

Notice how Repplier is beginning to broaden her argument. She is no longer talking only about making children's stories "safe," but of tampering with faith.

---

1 *A painting not unlike the Ghirlandaio that Repplier mentions, but in "Triumph," the slain babies are spotless and capped with haloes.*

been children in their time, and who look back with wistful delight upon the familiar figures who were their earliest friends, are entitled to an opinion in the case. How admirable was the "righteous rage" of Charles Lamb, when he wanted to buy some of these same brutal fairy stories for the little Coleridges, and could find nothing but the correct and commonplace literature which his whole soul abhorred! "Mrs. Barbauld's and Mrs. Trimmer's[1] nonsense lay in piles about," he wrote indignantly to papa Coleridge, "and have banished all the old classics of the nursery. Knowledge, insignificant and vapid as Mrs. Barbauld's books convey, must, it seems, come to a child in the shape of knowledge; and his empty noddle must be turned with conceit of his own powers when he has learnt that a horse is an animal, and that Billy is better than a horse, and such like; instead of that beautiful interest in wild tales which made the child a man, while all the time he suspected himself to be no bigger than a child."

Just such a wild tale, fantastic rather than beautiful, haunted Chateaubriand[2] all his life—the story of Count Combourg's wooden leg, which, three hundred years after its owner's death, was seen at night walking solemnly down the steep turret stairs, attended by a huge black cat. Not at all the kind of story we would select

---

1 Both were poets and children's writers of late-eighteenth and early-nineteenth century England. Barbauld had been a noted anti-slave-trade reformer whose poems had originally been well received by William Wordsworth and Samuel Taylor Coleridge. Trimmer was among the first children's writers to advocate the taming of children's literature.

2 French poet, considered to be the founder of Romanticism in French literature.

to tell a child nowadays. By no means! Even the little Chateaubriand heard it from peasant lips. Yet in after years, when he had fought the battle of life, and fought it with success; when he had grown gray, and illustrious, and disillusioned, and melancholy, what should come back to his mind, with its old pleasant flavor of terror and mystery, but the vision of Count Combourg's wooden leg taking its midnight constitutional, with the black cat stepping softly on before? So he notes it gravely down in his Memoirs, just as Scott notes in his diary the pranks of Whippity Stourie, the Scotch bogie that steals at night into open nursery windows; and just as Heine, in gay, sunlit Paris, recalls with joy the dark, sweet, sombre tales of the witch and fairy haunted forests of Germany.

These are impressions worth recording, and they are only a few out of many which may be gathered from similar sources. That which is vital in literature or tradition, which has survived the obscurity and wreckage of the past, whether as legend, or ballad, or mere nursery rhyme, has survived in right of some intrinsic merit of its own, and will not be snuffed out of existence by any of our precautionary or hygienic measures. We could not banish Bluebeard if we would. He is as immortal as Hamlet, and when hundreds of years shall have passed over this uncomfortably enlightened world, the children of the future— who, thank Heaven, can never, with all our efforts, be born grown up—will still tremble at the blood-stained key, and rejoice when the big brave brothers come galloping up the road.

We could not even rid ourselves of Mother Goose, though she, too, has her mortal enemies, who protest periodically against her cruelty and grossness. We could not drive Punch and Judy from our midst, though Mr. Punch's derelictions have been the subject of much serious and adverse criticism. It is not by such barbarous rhymes or by such brutal spectacles that we teach a child the lessons of integrity and gentleness, explain our nursery moralists, and probably they are correct. Moreover, Bluebeard does not teach a lesson of conjugal felicity, and Cinderella is full of the world's vanities, and Puss in Boots is one long record of triumphant effrontery and deception. An honest and self-respecting lad would have explained to the king that he was not the Marquis of Carabas at all; that he had no desire to profit by his cat's ingenious falsehoods, and no weak ambition to connect himself with the aristocracy. Such a hero would be a credit to our modern schoolrooms, and lift a load of care from the shoulders of our modern critics. Only the children would have none of him, but would turn wistfully back to those brave old tales which are their inheritance from a splendid past, and of which no hand shall rob them.

Agnes Repplier was a female essayist from Philadelphia, Pennsylvania. Born on April 1, 1855, she taught herself how to read at the age of ten and became an insatiable reader. She was a regular contributor of essays to The Atlantic Monthly *until 1940. During her long and successful career, she was awarded honorary doctor of letters degrees from Yale, Princeton, Columbia, and Temple University, and the University of Pennsylvania. She died on November 15, 1950, at the age of ninety-five.*

EXERCISE FOUR:

Answer the following questions about the essay, "Battle of the Babies." Be certain to base your answers on what the essay actually says and not on your reaction—either positive or negative—to the essay or the writer.

1. Toward what type of audience is this essay spun? How do you know?

_____

_____

_____

_____

_____

_____

_____

_____

_____

2. What is Repplier's purpose in quoting Lang's references to Cain, the Flood, David, and Henry VIII?

_____

_____

_____

_____

_____

_____

_____

_____

_____

3. What evidence of logical fallacy and/or propaganda can you find in this essay?

_____

_____

_____

_____

_____

_____

_____

_____

4. Can we conclude that this essay is biased? Why or why not?

_____

_____

_____

_____

_____

_____

_____

Writing Opportunity Two: Identify a social or political issue (*not* a philosophical view) about which you have an opinion. Gather whatever information you need to articulate and support that opinion and then write a strong editorial arguing your position. Remember that, while you are arguing a personal view or opinion, much of the strength of your editorial will lie in the integrity of your information and approach.

The page opposite the editorial page in a print newspaper is usually called the "op-ed" page and is dedicated to printing letters to the editor from the newspaper's readership. Again, many online journals, blogs, and newspapers allow—or even encourage—their readership to submit comments. Often, these letters to the editor respond to stories that have appeared earlier in the same journal—agreeing or disagreeing with the original writer's slant. Often, they are in response to previously published editorials or letters to the editor.

Why should a newspaper or e-journal's readers care to read the opinions of the other readers? Many don't, and many find themselves angered by the bias or the "stupidity" of readers whose opinions differ from their own. Still, many letters to the editor are written by experts in a particular field, who are able to provide additional information or insight, correct any misinformation in the original, or simply amplify the original writer's point. Many writers of letters to the editor have training or experience that puts them in a position to interpret events or express opinions that have more weight than other readers.

Whatever the case, the editors of the journals, in an effort to help their readers exercise their right to free speech, offer their op-ed pages as forums for the free exchange of ideas.

These pieces, as examples of nonfiction, tend to be a mixed bag of fact, interpretation, bias, opinion, and more. The foundation of both editorials and letters to the editor is either the editorial writer's interpretation of facts or events or his or her opinion. In well-respected journals, whether print or online, the writer's interpretation will be based on careful inquiry and close analysis. The writer's opinion will be well-founded in fact, training, and/or experience. There are always, of course, those newspapers, journals, blogs, and other sources—both print and electronic—that communicate only misinformation and the bias of the authors. It is, therefore, important to read editorials and letters to the editor with care, examining the credentials of the writer, the publication in which the piece is appearing, and whether or not the writer presents facts in support of his or her argument or merely asserts the argument.

Read the following two historically famous letters to the editor that represent two vastly different positions on the same topic. Notice how the writers of each blend opinion and fact and employ rhetorical and stylistic devices as well as potential propaganda techniques to establish the validity of their arguments.

Ultimately, which one is the more persuasive?

Why?

STATEMENT BY ALABAMA CLERGYMEN, APRIL 12, 1963

The following statement by eight white Alabama clergymen, reprinted by the American Friends Service Committee, prompted Martin Luther King, Jr.'s "Letter from Birmingham Jail."

What do you suppose the writers are trying to achieve by identifying themselves as clergymen at the absolute beginning of their letter to the editor?

Considering the time period in which this letter was written, the phrases "Law and Order" and "Common Sense" are charged with interpretation.

"Responsible citizens" is a very ambiguous term.

We the undersigned clergymen are among those who, in January, issued "An Appeal for Law and Order and Common Sense," in dealing with racial problems in Alabama. We expressed understanding that honest convictions in racial matters could properly be pursued in the courts, but urged that decisions of those courts should in the meantime be peacefully obeyed.

Since that time there had been some evidence of increased forbearance and a willingness to face facts. Responsible citizens have undertaken to work on various problems which cause racial friction and unrest. In Birmingham, recent public events have given indication that we will have opportunity for a new constructive and realistic approach to racial problems.

However, we are now confronted by a series of demonstrations by some of our Negro citizens, directed and led in part by outsiders. We recognize the natural impatience of people who feel that their hopes are slow in being realized. But we are convinced that these demonstrations are unwise and untimely.

We agree rather with certain local Negro leadership which has called for honest and open negotiation of racial issues in our area. And we believe this kind of facing of issues can best be accomplished by citizens of our own metropolitan area, white and Negro, meeting with their knowledge and experience of the local situation. All of us need to face that responsibility and find proper channels for its accomplishment.

Just as we formerly pointed out that "hatred and violence have no sanction in our religious and political traditions," we also point out that such actions as incite to hatred and violence, however technically peaceful those actions may be, have not contributed to the resolution of our local problems. We do not believe that these days of new hope are days when extreme measures are justified in Birmingham.

We commend the community as a whole, and the local news media and law enforcement officials in particular, on the calm manner in which these demonstrations have been handled. We urge the public to continue to show restraint should the demonstrations continue, and the law enforcement officials to remain calm and continue to protect our city from violence.

We further strongly urge our own Negro community to withdraw support from these demonstrations, and to unite locally in working peacefully for a better Birmingham. When rights are consistently denied, a cause should be pressed in the courts and in negotiations among local leaders, and not in the streets. We appeal to both

Notice that the writers contrast the local leadership—by implication, the "responsible citizens" mentioned in the paragraph before the previous one—and the "outsiders" who are leading the demonstrations mentioned in the previous paragraph.

Notice that the writers of this letter do not reference any specific actions or persons.

"Calm" and "restraint" are interpretive, not factual, terms.

143

The letter is well structured, returning to essentially the same point on which it began, "law and order and common sense."

our white and Negro citizenry to observe the principles of law and order and common sense.

Signed by:

C.C.J. Carpenter, D.D., LL.D., Bishop of Alabama

Joseph A. Durick, D.D., Auxiliary Bishop, Diocese of Mobile-Birmingham

Rabbi Milton L. Grafman, Temple Emanu-El, Birmingham, Alabama

Bishop Paul Hardin, Bishop of the Alabama-West Florida Conference of the Methodist Church

Bishop Nolan B. Harmon, Bishop of the North Alabama Conference of the Methodist Church

George M. Murray, D.D., LL.D., Bishop Coadjutor, Episcopal Diocese of Alabama

Edward V. Ramage, Moderator, Synod of the Alabama Presbyterian Church in the United States

Earl Stallings, Pastor, First Baptist Church, Birmingham, Alabama

LETTER FROM BIRMINGHAM JAIL, APRIL 16, 1963

This letter was written on April 16, 1963, in response to the April 12, 1963, Statement by Alabama Clergymen. It was first published in The Christian Century, *June 1, 1963. Notice how the author, Rev. Dr. Martin Luther King, Jr., addresses the Alabama clergymen's arguments.*

*AUTHOR'S NOTE: This response to a published statement by eight fellow clergymen from Alabama (Bishop C. C. J. Carpenter, Bishop Joseph A. Durick, Rabbi Hilton L. Grafman, Bishop Paul Hardin, Bishop Holan B. Harmon, the Reverend George M. Murray. the Reverend Edward V. Ramage and the Reverend Earl Stallings) was composed under somewhat constricting circumstance. Begun on the margins of the newspaper in which the statement appeared while I was in jail, the letter was continued on scraps of writing paper supplied by a friendly Negro trusty, and concluded on a pad my attorneys were eventually permitted to leave me. Although the text remains in substance unaltered, I have indulged in the author's prerogative of polishing it for publication.

My Dear Fellow Clergymen:

While confined here in the Birmingham city jail, I came across your recent statement calling my present activities "unwise and untimely." Seldom do I pause to answer criticism of my work and ideas. If I sought to answer all the criticisms that cross my desk, my secretaries would have little time for anything other than such correspondence in the course of the day, and I would have no time for constructive work. But since I feel that you are men of genuine good will and that your criticisms are sincerely set forth, I want to try to answer your statements in what I hope will be patient and reasonable terms.

I think I should indicate why I am here in Birmingham, since you have been influenced by the view which argues against "outsiders coming in." I have the honor of serving as president of the Southern Christian Leadership Conference, an organization operating in every southern state, with headquarters in Atlanta, Georgia. We have some eighty-five affiliated organizations across the South, and one of them is the Alabama Christian Movement for Human Rights. Frequently we share staff, educational and financial resources with our affiliates. Several months ago the affiliate here in Birmingham asked us to be on call to engage in a nonviolent direct-action program if such were deemed necessary. We readily consented, and when the hour came we lived up to our promise. So I, along with several members of my staff, am here because I was invited here. I am here because I have organizational ties here.

But more basically, I am in Birmingham because injustice is here. Just as the prophets of the eighth century B.C. left their villages and carried their "thus saith the Lord" far beyond the boundaries of their home towns, and just as the Apostle Paul left his village of Tarsus and carried the gospel of Jesus Christ to the far corners of

the Greco-Roman world, so am I compelled to
carry the gospel of freedom beyond my own
home town. Like Paul, I must constantly respond
to the Macedonian call for aid. Moreover, I
am cognizant of the interrelatedness of all
communities and states. I cannot sit idly by
in Atlanta and not be concerned about what
happens in Birmingham. Injustice anywhere is a
threat to justice everywhere. We are caught in an
inescapable network of mutuality, tied in a single
garment of destiny. Whatever affects one directly,
affects all indirectly. Never again can we afford to
live with the narrow, provincial "outside agitator"
idea. Anyone who lives inside the United States
can never be considered an outsider anywhere
within its bounds.

You deplore the demonstrations taking place
in Birmingham. But your statement, I am
sorry to say, fails to express a similar concern
for the conditions that brought about the
demonstrations. I am sure that none of you
would want to rest content with the superficial
kind of social analysis that deals merely with
effects and does not grapple with underlying
causes. It is unfortunate that demonstrations are
taking place in Birmingham, but it is even more
unfortunate that the city's white power structure
left the Negro community with no alternative.

In any nonviolent campaign there are four
basic steps: collection of the facts to determine
whether injustices exist; negotiation; self-
purification; and direct action. We have gone
through all of these steps in Birmingham.
There can be no gainsaying the fact that racial
injustice engulfs this community. Birmingham is
probably the most thoroughly segregated city in

the United States. Its ugly record of brutality is widely known. Negroes have experienced grossly unjust treatment in the courts. There have been more unsolved bombings of Negro homes and churches in Birmingham than in any other city in the nation. These are the hard, brutal facts of the case. On the basis of these conditions, Negro leaders sought to negotiate with the city fathers. But the latter consistently refused to engage in good-faith negotiation.

Then, last September, came the opportunity to talk with leaders of Birmingham's economic community. In the course of the negotiations, certain promises were made by the merchants— for example, to remove the stores' humiliating racial signs. On the basis of these promises, the Reverend Fred Shuttlesworth and the leaders of the Alabama Christian Movement for Human Rights agreed to a moratorium on all demonstrations. As the weeks and months went by, we realized that we were the victims of a broken promise. A few signs, briefly removed, returned; the others remained. As in so many past experiences, our hopes had been blasted, and the shadow of deep disappointment settled upon us. We had no alternative except to prepare for direct action, whereby we would present our very bodies as a means of laying our case before the conscience of the local and the national community. Mindful of the difficulties involved, we decided to undertake a process of self-purification. We began a series of workshops on nonviolence, and we repeatedly asked ourselves: "Are you able to accept blows without retaliating?" "Are you able to endure the ordeal of jail?" We decided to schedule our direct-action program for the Easter season, realizing that except for Christmas, this is the main shopping period of the year. Knowing that a strong economic withdrawal program would be the by-product of direct action, we felt that this would be the best time to bring pressure to bear on the merchants for the needed change.

Then it occurred to us that Birmingham's mayoralty election was coming up in March, and we speedily decided to postpone action until after election day. When we discovered that the Commissioner of Public Safety, Eugene "Bull" Connor, had piled up enough votes to be in the run-off we decided again to postpone action until the day after the run-off so that the demonstrations could not be used to cloud the issues. Like many others, we waited to see Mr. Connor defeated, and to this end we endured postponement after postponement. Having aided in this community need, we felt that our direct-action program could be delayed no longer.

You may well ask: "Why direct action? Why sit-ins, marches and so forth? Isn't negotiation a better path?" You are quite right in calling for negotiation. Indeed, this is the very purpose of direct action. Nonviolent direct action seeks to create such a crisis and foster such a tension that a community which has constantly refused to negotiate is forced to confront the issue. It seeks to so dramatize the issue that it can no longer be ignored. My citing the creation of tension as part of the work of the nonviolent-resister may sound rather shocking. But I must confess that I am not afraid of the word "tension." I have earnestly opposed violent tension, but there is a type of constructive, nonviolent tension which is necessary for growth. Just as Socrates felt that it

Anticipating a reader's potential objections and addressing them directly is a rhetorical device called *procatalepsis*.

Another example of procatalepsis.

was necessary to create a tension in the mind so
that individuals could rise from the bondage of
myths and half-truths to the unfettered realm of
creative analysis and objective appraisal, so must
we see the need for nonviolent gadflies to create
the kind of tension in society that will help
men rise from the dark depths of prejudice and
racism to the majestic heights of understanding
and brotherhood.

The purpose of our direct-action program is
to create a situation so crisis-packed that it
will inevitably open the door to negotiation.
I therefore concur with you in your call for
negotiation. Too long has our beloved Southland
been bogged down in a tragic effort to live in
monologue rather than dialogue.

One of the basic points in your statement is that
the action that I and my associates have taken in
Birmingham is untimely. Some have asked: "Why
didn't you give the new city administration time
to act?" The only answer that I can give to this
query is that the new Birmingham administration
must be prodded about as much as the
outgoing one, before it will act. We are sadly
mistaken if we feel that the election of Albert
Boutwell as mayor will bring the millennium
to Birmingham. While Mr. Boutwell is a much
more gentle person than Mr. Connor, they are
both segregationists, dedicated to maintenance
of the status quo. I have hope that Mr. Boutwell
will be reasonable enough to see the futility of
massive resistance to desegregation. But he will
not see this without pressure from devotees
of civil rights. My friends, I must say to you
that we have not made a single civil rights
gain without determined legal and nonviolent

pressure. Lamentably, it is an historical fact that privileged groups seldom give up their privileges voluntarily. Individuals may see the moral light and voluntarily give up their unjust posture; but, as Reinhold Niebuhr has reminded us, groups tend to be more immoral than individuals.

We know through painful experience that freedom is never voluntarily given by the oppressor; it must be demanded by the oppressed. Frankly, I have yet to engage in a direct-action campaign that was "well timed" in the view of those who have not suffered unduly from the disease of segregation. For years now I have heard the word "Wait!" It rings in the ear of every Negro with piercing familiarity. This "Wait" has almost always meant "Never." We must come to see, with one of our distinguished jurists, that "justice too long delayed is justice denied."

We have waited for more than 340 years for our constitutional and God-given rights. The nations of Asia and Africa are moving with jetlike speed toward gaining political independence, but we still creep at horse-and-buggy pace toward gaining a cup of coffee at a lunch counter. Perhaps it is easy for those who have never felt the stinging dark of segregation to say, "Wait." But when you have seen vicious mobs lynch your mothers and fathers at will and drown your sisters and brothers at whim; when you have seen hate-filled policemen curse, kick and even kill your black brothers and sisters; when you see the vast majority of your twenty million Negro brothers smothering in an airtight cage of poverty in the midst of an affluent society; when you suddenly find your tongue twisted and your speech stammering as you seek to explain to your six-year-old daughter why she can't go to the public amusement park that has just been advertised on television, and see tears welling up in her eyes when she is told that Funtown is closed to colored children, and see ominous clouds of inferiority beginning to form in her little mental sky, and see her beginning to distort her personality by developing an unconscious bitterness toward white people; when you have to concoct an answer for a five-year-old son who is asking: "Daddy, why do white people treat colored people so mean?"; when you take a cross-country drive and find it necessary to sleep night after night in the uncomfortable corners of your automobile because no motel will accept you; when you are humiliated day in and day out by nagging signs reading "white" and "colored"; when your first name becomes "nigger," your middle name becomes "boy" (however old you are) and your last name becomes "John," and your wife and mother are never given the respected title "Mrs."; when you are harried by day and haunted by night by the fact that you are a Negro, living constantly at tiptoe stance, never quite knowing what to expect next, and are plagued with inner fears and outer resentments; when you go forever fighting a degenerating sense of "nobodiness" then you will understand why we find it difficult to wait. There comes a time when the cup of endurance runs over, and men are no longer willing to be plunged into the abyss of despair. I hope, sirs, you can understand our legitimate and unavoidable impatience.

You express a great deal of anxiety over our willingness to break laws. This is certainly a legitimate concern. Since we so diligently urge people to obey the Supreme Court's decision of 1954 outlawing segregation in the public schools, at first glance it may seem rather paradoxical for us consciously to break laws. One may want to ask: "How can you advocate breaking some laws and obeying others?" The answer lies in the fact that there are two types of laws: just and unjust. I would be the first to advocate obeying just laws. One has not only a legal but a moral responsibility to obey just laws. Conversely, one has a moral responsibility to disobey unjust laws. I would agree with St. Augustine that "an unjust law is no law at all"

Now, what is the difference between the two? How does one determine whether a law is just or unjust? A just law is a man-made code that squares with the moral law or the law of God. An unjust law is a code that is out of harmony with the moral law. To put it in the terms of St. Thomas Aquinas: An unjust law is a human law that is not rooted in eternal law and natural law. Any law that uplifts human personality is just. Any law that degrades human personality is unjust. All segregation statutes are unjust because segregation distorts the soul and damages the personality. It gives the segregator a false sense of superiority and the segregated a false sense of inferiority. Segregation, to use the terminology of the Jewish philosopher Martin Buber, substitutes an "I-it" relationship for an "I-thou" relationship and ends up relegating persons to the status of things. Hence segregation is not only politically, economically and sociologically unsound, it is morally wrong and awful. Paul Tillich said that sin is separation. Is not segregation an existential expression "of man's tragic separation, his awful estrangement, his terrible sinfulness?" Thus it is that I can urge men to obey the 1954 decision of the Supreme Court, for it is morally right; and I can urge them to disobey segregation ordinances, for they are morally wrong.

Let us consider a more concrete example of just and unjust laws. An unjust law is a code that a numerical or power majority group compels a minority group to obey but does not make binding on itself. This is difference made legal. By the same token, a just law is a code that a majority compels a minority to follow and that it is willing to follow itself. This is sameness made legal.

Let me give another explanation. A law is unjust if it is inflicted on a minority that, as a result of being denied the right to vote, had no part in enacting or devising the law. Who can say that the legislature of Alabama which set up that state's segregation laws was democratically elected? Throughout Alabama all sorts of devious methods are used to prevent Negroes from becoming registered voters, and there are some counties in which, even though Negroes constitute a majority of the population, not a single Negro is registered. Can any law enacted under such circumstances be considered democratically structured?

Sometimes a law is just on its face and unjust in its application. For instance, I have been arrested on a charge of parading without a permit. Now, there is nothing wrong in having an ordinance which requires a permit for a parade. But such an ordinance becomes unjust when it is used to maintain segregation and to deny citizens the First Amendment privilege of peaceful assembly and protest.

I hope you are able to see the distinction I am trying to point out. In no sense do I advocate evading or defying the law, as would the rabid segregationist. That would lead to anarchy. One who breaks an unjust law must do so openly, lovingly, and with a willingness to accept the penalty. I submit that an individual who breaks a law that conscience tells him is unjust and who willingly accepts the penalty of imprisonment in order to arouse the conscience of the community over its injustice, is in reality expressing the highest respect for law.

Of course, there is nothing new about this kind of civil disobedience. It was evidenced sublimely in the refusal of Shadrach, Meshach and Abednego to obey the laws of Nebuchadnezzar, on the ground that a higher moral law was at stake. It was practiced superbly by the early Christians, who were willing to face hungry lions and the excruciating pain of chopping blocks rather than submit to certain unjust laws of the Roman Empire. To a degree, academic freedom is a reality today because Socrates practiced civil disobedience. In our own nation, the Boston Tea Party represented a massive act of civil disobedience.

We should never forget that everything Adolf Hitler did in Germany was "legal" and everything the Hungarian freedom fighters did in Hungary was "illegal." It was "illegal" to aid and comfort a Jew in Hitler's Germany. Even so, I am sure that, had I lived in Germany at the time, I would have aided and comforted my Jewish brothers. If today I lived in a Communist country where certain principles dear to the Christian faith are suppressed, I would openly advocate disobeying that country's antireligious laws.

I must make two honest confessions to you, my Christian and Jewish brothers. First, I must confess that over the past few years I have been gravely disappointed with the white moderate. I have almost reached the regrettable conclusion that the Negro's great stumbling block in his stride toward freedom is not the White Citizen's Counciler or the Ku Klux Klanner, but the white moderate, who is more devoted to "order" than to justice; who prefers a negative peace which is the absence of tension to a positive peace which is the presence of justice; who constantly says: "I agree with you in the goal you seek, but I cannot agree with your methods of direct action"; who paternalistically believes he can set the timetable for another man's freedom; who lives by a mythical concept of time and who constantly advises the Negro to wait for a "more convenient season." Shallow understanding from people of good will is more frustrating than absolute misunderstanding from people of ill will. Lukewarm acceptance is much more bewildering than outright rejection.

> The juxtaposition of two contrasting ideas like this is a rhetorical device known as *antithesis.*

> Two more examples of antithesis.

I had hoped that the white moderate would understand that law and order exist for the purpose of establishing justice and that when they fail in this purpose they become the dangerously structured dams that block the flow of social progress. I had hoped that the white moderate would understand that the present tension in the South is a necessary phase of the transition from an obnoxious negative peace, in which the Negro passively accepted his unjust plight, to a substantive and positive peace, in which all men will respect the dignity and worth of human personality. Actually, we who engage in nonviolent direct action are not the creators

> The repetition of words at the beginning of successive sentences is another rhetorical device known as *anaphora.* It was a favorite device of King's, and he uses it elsewhere in this letter.

of tension. We merely bring to the surface the hidden tension that is already alive. We bring it out in the open, where it can be seen and dealt with. Like a boil that can never be cured so long as it is covered up but must be opened with all its ugliness to the natural medicines of air and light, injustice must be exposed, with all the tension its exposure creates, to the light of human conscience and the air of national opinion before it can be cured.

In your statement you assert that our actions, even though peaceful, must be condemned because they precipitate violence. But is this a logical assertion? Isn't this like condemning a robbed man because his possession of money precipitated the evil act of robbery? Isn't this like condemning Socrates because his unswerving commitment to truth and his philosophical inquiries precipitated the act by the misguided populace in which they made him drink hemlock? Isn't this like condemning Jesus because his unique God-consciousness and never-ceasing devotion to God's will precipitated the evil act of crucifixion? We must come to see that, as the federal courts have consistently affirmed, it is wrong to urge an individual to cease his efforts to gain his basic constitutional rights because the quest may precipitate violence. Society must protect the robbed and punish the robber.

I had also hoped that the white moderate would reject the myth concerning time in relation to the struggle for freedom. I have just received a letter from a white brother in Texas. He writes: "All Christians know that the colored people will receive equal rights eventually, but it is possible that you are in too great a religious hurry. It has taken Christianity almost two thousand years to accomplish what it has. The teachings of Christ take time to come to earth." Such an attitude stems from a tragic misconception of time, from the strangely rational notion that there is something in the very flow of time that will inevitably cure all ills. Actually, time itself is neutral; it can be used either destructively or constructively. More and more I feel that the people of ill will have used time much more effectively than have the people of good will. We will have to repent in this generation not merely for the hateful words and actions of the bad people but for the appalling silence of the good people. Human progress never rolls in on wheels of inevitability; it comes through the tireless efforts of men willing to be co-workers with God, and without this hard work, time itself becomes an ally of the forces of social stagnation. We must use time creatively, in the knowledge that the time is always ripe to do right. Now is the time to make real the promise of democracy and transform our pending national elegy into a creative psalm of brotherhood. Now is the time to lift our national policy from the quicksand of racial injustice to the solid rock of human dignity.

You speak of our activity in Birmingham as extreme. At fist I was rather disappointed that fellow clergymen would see my nonviolent efforts as those of an extremist. I began thinking about the fact that I stand in the middle of two opposing forces in the Negro community. One is a force of complacency, made up in part of Negroes who, as a result of long years of oppression, are so drained of self-respect and a sense of "somebodiness" that they have adjusted to segregation; and in part of a few middle class Negroes who, because of a degree of academic and economic security and because in some ways they profit by segregation, have become insensitive to the problems of the masses. The other force is one of bitterness and hatred, and it comes perilously close to advocating violence. It is expressed in the various black nationalist groups that are springing up across the nation, the largest and best-known being Elijah Muhammad's Muslim movement. Nourished by the Negro's frustration over the continued existence of racial discrimination, this movement is made up of people who have lost faith in America, who have absolutely repudiated Christianity, and who have concluded that the white man is an incorrigible "devil."

I have tried to stand between these two forces, saying that we need emulate neither the "do-nothingism" of the complacent nor the hatred and despair of the black nationalist. For there is the more excellent way of love and nonviolent protest. I am grateful to God that, through the influence of the Negro church, the way of nonviolence became an integral part of our struggle.

If this philosophy had not emerged, by now many streets of the South would, I am convinced, be flowing with blood. And I am further convinced that if our white brothers dismiss as "rabble-rousers" and "outside agitators" those of us who employ nonviolent direct action, and if they refuse to support our nonviolent efforts, millions of Negroes will, out of frustration and despair, seek solace and security in black-nationalist ideologies a development that would inevitably lead to a frightening racial nightmare.

Oppressed people cannot remain oppressed forever. The yearning for freedom eventually manifests itself, and that is what has happened to the American Negro. Something within has reminded him of his birthright of freedom, and something without has reminded him that it can be gained. Consciously or unconsciously, he has been caught up by the Zeitgeist, and with his black brothers of Africa and his brown and yellow brothers of Asia, South America and the Caribbean, the United States Negro is moving with a sense of great urgency toward the promised land of racial justice. If one recognizes this vital urge that has engulfed the Negro community, one should readily understand why public demonstrations are taking place. The Negro has many pent-up resentments and latent frustrations, and he must release them. So let him march; let him make prayer pilgrimages to the city hall; let him go on freedom rides—and try to understand why he must do so. If his repressed emotions are not released in nonviolent ways, they will seek expression through violence; this is not a threat but a fact of history. So I have not said to my people: "Get rid of your discontent." Rather, I have tried to say that this normal and healthy discontent can be channeled into the creative outlet of nonviolent direct action. And now this approach is being termed extremist.

But though I was initially disappointed at being categorized as an extremist, as I continued to think about the matter I gradually gained a measure of satisfaction from the label. Was not Jesus an extremist for love: "Love your enemies, bless them that curse you, do good to them that hate you, and pray for them which despitefully use you, and persecute you." Was not Amos an extremist for justice: "Let justice roll down like waters and righteousness like an ever-flowing stream." Was not Paul an extremist for the Christian gospel: "I bear in my body the marks of the Lord Jesus." Was not Martin Luther an extremist: "Here I stand; I cannot do otherwise, so help me God." And John Bunyan: "I will stay in jail to the end of my days before I make a butchery of my conscience." And Abraham Lincoln: "This nation cannot survive half slave and half free." And Thomas Jefferson: "We hold these truths to be self-evident, that all men are created equal ..." So the question is not whether we will be extremists, but what kind of extremists we will be. Will we be extremists for hate or for love? Will we be extremists for the preservation of injustice or for the extension of justice? In that dramatic scene on Calvary's hill three men were crucified. We must never forget that all three were crucified for the same crime—-the crime of extremism. Two were extremists for immorality, and thus fell below their environment. The other, Jesus Christ, was an extremist for love, truth and goodness, and thereby rose above his environment. Perhaps the South, the nation and the world are in dire need of creative extremists.

I had hoped that the white moderate would see this need. Perhaps I was too optimistic; perhaps I expected too much. I suppose I should have realized that few members of the oppressor race can understand the deep groans and passionate yearnings of the oppressed race, and still fewer have the vision to see that injustice must be

Notice that King is still echoing his earlier anaphora.

rooted out by strong, persistent and determined action. I am thankful, however, that some of our white brothers in the South have grasped the meaning of this social revolution and committed themselves to it. They are still too few in quantity, but they are big in quality. Some—such as Ralph McGill, Lillian Smith, Harry Golden, James McBride Dabbs, Ann Braden and Sarah Patton Boyle—have written about our struggle in eloquent and prophetic terms. Others have marched with us down nameless streets of the South. They have languished in filthy, roach-infested jails, suffering the abuse and brutality of policemen who view them as "dirty nigger lovers." Unlike so many of their moderate brothers and sisters, they have recognized the urgency of the moment and sensed the need for powerful "action" antidotes to combat the disease of segregation.

Let me take note of my other major disappointment. I have been so greatly disappointed with the white church and its leadership. Of course, there are some notable exceptions. I am not unmindful of the fact that each of you has taken some significant stands on this issue. I commend you, Reverend Stallings, for your Christian stand on this past Sunday, in welcoming Negroes to your worship service on a non segregated basis. I commend the Catholic leaders of this state for integrating Spring Hill College several years ago.

But despite these notable exceptions, I must honestly reiterate that I have been disappointed with the church. I do not say this as one of those negative critics who can always find something wrong with the church. I say this as a minister of the gospel, who loves the church; who was nurtured in its bosom; who has been sustained by its spiritual blessings and who will remain true to it as long as the cord of Rio shall lengthen.

When I was suddenly catapulted into the leadership of the bus protest in Montgomery, Alabama, a few years ago, I felt we would be supported by the white church. I felt that the white ministers, priests and rabbis of the South would be among our strongest allies. Instead, some have been outright opponents, refusing to understand the freedom movement and misrepresenting its leader era; all too many others have been more cautious than courageous and have remained silent behind the anesthetizing security of stained-glass windows. In spite of my shattered dreams, I came to Birmingham with the hope that the white religious leadership of this community would see the justice of our cause and, with deep moral concern, would serve as the channel through which our just grievances could reach the power structure. I had hoped that each of you would understand. But again I have been disappointed.

I have heard numerous southern religious leaders admonish their worshipers to comply with a desegregation decision because it is the law, but I have longed to hear white ministers declare: "Follow this decree because integration is morally right and because the Negro is your brother." In the midst of blatant injustices inflicted upon the Negro, I have watched white churchmen stand on the sideline and mouth pious irrelevancies and sanctimonious trivialities. In the midst of a mighty struggle to rid our nation of racial and economic injustice, I have heard many ministers say: "Those are social issues, with which the gospel has no real concern." And I have watched many churches commit themselves to a completely other worldly religion which makes a strange, un-Biblical distinction between body and soul, between the sacred and the secular.

I have traveled the length and breadth of Alabama, Mississippi and all the other southern states. On sweltering summer days and crisp autumn mornings I have looked at the South's beautiful churches with their lofty spires pointing heavenward. I have beheld the impressive outlines of her massive religious-education buildings. Over and over I have found myself asking: "What kind of people worship here? Who is their God? Where were their voices when the lips of Governor Barnett dripped with words of interposition and nullification? Where were they when Governor Wallace gave a clarion call for defiance and hatred? Where were their voices of support when bruised and weary Negro men and women decided to rise from the dark dungeons of complacency to the bright hills of creative protest?"

Yes, these questions are still in my mind. In deep disappointment I have wept over the laxity of the church. But be assured that my tears have been tears of love. There can be no deep disappointment where there is not deep love. Yes, I love the church. How could I do otherwise? I am in the rather unique position of being the son, the grandson and the great-grandson of preachers. Yes, I see the church as the body of Christ. But, oh! How we have blemished and scarred that body through social neglect and through fear of being nonconformists.

There was a time when the church was very powerful in the time when the early Christians rejoiced at being deemed worthy to suffer for what they believed. In those days the church was not merely a thermometer that recorded the ideas and principles of popular opinion; it was a thermostat that transformed the mores of society. Whenever the early Christians entered a town, the people in power became disturbed and immediately sought to convict the Christians for being "disturbers of the peace" and "outside agitators." But the Christians pressed on, in the conviction that they were "a colony of heaven," called to obey God rather than man. Small in number, they were big in commitment. They were too God intoxicated to be "astronomically intimidated." By their effort and example they brought an end to such ancient evils as infanticide and gladiatorial contests.

Things are different now. So often the contemporary church is a weak, ineffectual voice with an uncertain sound. So often it is an archdefender of the status quo. Far from being disturbed by the presence of the church, the power structure of the average community is consoled by the church's silent and often even vocal sanction of things as they are.

But the judgment of God is upon the church as never before. If today's church does not recapture the sacrificial spirit of the early church, it will lose its authenticity, forfeit the loyalty of millions, and be dismissed as an irrelevant social club with

no meaning for the twentieth century. Every day
I meet young people whose disappointment with
the church has turned into outright disgust.

Perhaps I have once again been too optimistic.
Is organized religion too inextricably bound to
the status quo to save our nation and the world?
Perhaps I must turn my faith to the inner spiritual
church, the church within the church, as the true
ecclesia and the hope of the world. But again I
am thankful to God that some noble souls from
the ranks of organized religion have broken loose
from the paralyzing chains of conformity and
joined us as active partners in the struggle for
freedom. They have left their secure congregations
and walked the streets of Albany, Georgia, with
us. They have gone down the highways of the
South on tortuous rides for freedom. Yes, they
have gone to jail with us. Some have been
dismissed from their churches, have lost the
support of their bishops and fellow ministers. But
they have acted in the faith that right defeated is
stronger than evil triumphant. Their witness has
been the spiritual salt that has preserved the true
meaning of the gospel in these troubled times.
They have carved a tunnel of hope through the
dark mountain of disappointment.

I hope the church as a whole will meet the
challenge of this decisive hour. But even if the
church does not come to the aid of justice, I have
no despair about the future. I have no fear about
the outcome of our struggle in Birmingham, even
if our motives are at present misunderstood. We
will reach the goal of freedom in Birmingham and
all over the nation, because the goal of America
is freedom. Abused and scorned though we
may be, our destiny is tied up with America's

destiny. Before the pilgrims landed at Plymouth, we were here. Before the pen of Jefferson etched the majestic words of the Declaration of Independence across the pages of history, we were here. For more than two centuries our forebears labored in this country without wages; they made cotton king; they built the homes of their masters while suffering gross injustice and shameful humiliation—and yet out of a bottomless vitality they continued to thrive and develop. If the inexpressible cruelties of slavery could not stop us, the opposition we now face will surely fail. We will win our freedom because the sacred heritage of our nation and the eternal will of God are embodied in our echoing demands.

Before closing I feel impelled to mention one other point in your statement that has troubled me profoundly. You warmly commended the Birmingham police force for keeping "order" and "preventing violence." I doubt that you would have so warmly commended the police force if you had seen its dogs sinking their teeth into unarmed, nonviolent Negroes. I doubt that you would so quickly commend the policemen if you were to observe their ugly and inhumane treatment of Negroes here in the city jail; if you were to watch them push and curse old Negro women and young Negro girls; if you were to see them slap and kick old Negro men and young boys; if you were to observe them, as they did on two occasions, refuse to give us food because we wanted to sing our grace together. I cannot join you in your praise of the Birmingham police department.

It is true that the police have exercised a degree of discipline in handling the demonstrators. In this sense they have conducted themselves rather "nonviolently" in public. But for what purpose? To preserve the evil system of segregation. Over the past few years I have consistently preached that nonviolence demands that the means we use must be as pure as the ends we seek. I have tried to make clear that it is wrong to use immoral means to attain moral ends. But now I must affirm that it is just as wrong, or perhaps even more so, to use moral means to preserve immoral ends. Perhaps Mr. Connor and his policemen have been rather nonviolent in public, as was Chief Pritchett in Albany, Georgia, but they have used the moral means of nonviolence to maintain the immoral end of racial injustice. As T. S. Eliot has said: "The last temptation is the greatest treason: To do the right deed for the wrong reason."

I wish you had commended the Negro sit-inners and demonstrators of Birmingham for their sublime courage, their willingness to suffer and their amazing discipline in the midst of great provocation. One day the South will recognize its real heroes. There will be the James Merediths, with the noble sense of purpose that enables them to face jeering and hostile mobs, and with the agonizing loneliness that characterizes the life of the pioneer. There will be the old, oppressed, battered Negro women, symbolized in a seventy-two-year-old woman in Montgomery, Alabama, who rose up with a sense of dignity and with her people decided not to ride segregated buses, and who responded with ungrammatical profundity to one who inquired about her weariness: "My feets is tired, but my soul is at rest." There will be the young high school and college students, the young ministers of the gospel and a host of their elders, courageously and nonviolently sitting in at lunch counters and willingly going to jail for conscience' sake. One day the South will know that when these disinherited children of God sat down at lunch counters, they were in reality standing up for what is best in the American dream and for the most sacred values in our Judaeo-Christian heritage, thereby bringing our nation back to those great wells of democracy which were dug deep by the founding fathers in their formulation of the Constitution and the Declaration of Independence.

Never before have I written so long a letter. I'm afraid it is much too long to take your precious time. I can assure you that it would have been much shorter if I had been writing from a comfortable desk, but what else can one do when he is alone in a narrow jail cell, other than write long letters, think long thoughts and pray long prayers?

If I have said anything in this letter that overstates the truth and indicates an unreasonable impatience, I beg you to forgive me. If I have said anything that understates the truth and indicates my having a patience that allows me to settle for anything less than brotherhood, I beg God to forgive me.

I hope this letter finds you strong in the faith. I also hope that circumstances will soon make it possible for me to meet each of you, not as an integrationist or a civil rights leader but as a fellow clergyman and a Christian brother. Let us all hope that the dark clouds of racial prejudice will soon pass away and the deep fog of misunderstanding will be lifted from our fear-drenched communities, and in some not too distant tomorrow the radiant stars of love and brotherhood will shine over our great nation with all their scintillating beauty.

Yours for the cause of Peace and Brotherhood,

Martin Luther King, Jr.

Martin Luther King, Jr. (1929–1968) was an American Baptist minister and a prominent leader in the African American civil rights movement. His 1963 "I Have a Dream" speech, delivered from the steps of the Lincoln Memorial in Washington, D.C., helped establish him as one of the greatest orators in United States history. In 1964, he became the youngest person ever to win the Nobel Peace Prize. He was assassinated in Memphis, Tennessee, on April 4, 1968.

EXERCISE FIVE:

Answer the following questions about "Letter from Birmingham Jail." Be certain to base your answers on what the letter actually says and not on your reaction—either positive or negative—to the editorial or the man who wrote it.

1. Who is King's specified audience? What is the immediate context in which this letter was written?

_____

_____

_____

_____

_____

_____

_____

_____

_____

2. What is the effect of King's using the words "criticism" and "constructive work" in the same sentence in the first paragraph?

_____

_____

_____

_____

_____

_____

_____

_____

3. How does King, jailed and accused of being an outside agitator, assuage potentially hostile responses to his letter?

_____

_____

_____

_____

_____

_____

_____

_____

4. What are the rhetorical purposes of the second paragraph?

_____

_____

_____

_____

_____

_____

_____

_____

5. What is King hoping to achieve by comparing himself and his work to the prophets and the Apostle Paul? Why does he choose these specific similes?

_____

_____

_____

_____

_____

_____

_____

_____

6. Of what flaw in reasoning does King accuse the local pastors in the fourth paragraph? What is the logical consequence of this flaw?

_____

_____

_____

_____

_____

_____

_____

_____

_____

7. Is King's statement, "There can be no gainsaying the fact that…" an example of a self-evident truth? Why or why not?

_____

_____

_____

_____

_____

_____

_____

_____

_____

_____

8. List some emotion-laden words and phrases King uses in the sixth paragraph. Why does he use a rhetorical technique that is often regarded as propagandistic?

_____

_____

_____

_____

_____

_____

_____

_____

_____

_____

9. Analyze King's statement, "My friends, I must say to you that we have not made a single civil rights gain without determined legal and nonviolent pressure." What is the purpose of the direct address? Is it an example of a self-evident truth or an unsupported claim?

10. Analyze the structure, language, and impact of the sentence in the twelfth paragraph that begins, "But when you have seen vicious mobs," and ends, "we find it difficult to wait."

_____

_____

_____

_____

_____

_____

_____

_____

_____

_____

_____

_____

_____

_____

_____

_____

_____

_____

_____

11. What is King's purpose in referring to St. Augustine, Martin Buber, and Paul
    Tillich? What has changed in the nature of King's argument?

    _____

    _____

    _____

    _____

    _____

    _____

    _____

    _____

12. Trace King's progression of ideas and examples of just versus unjust laws
    beginning in the fourteenth paragraph. Why is this progression effective?

    _____

    _____

    _____

    _____

    _____

    _____

    _____

    _____

    _____

13. Of what logical fallacy/propaganda technique does King accuse others in the African American community? How legitimate is his accusation?

_____

_____

_____

_____

_____

_____

_____

_____

_____

14. How do the style, structure, and tone of the letter's last several paragraphs differ from the style, structure, and tone of the earlier portions? Why?

_____

_____

_____

_____

_____

_____

_____

_____

_____

15. With what rhetorical appeals does King end the letter? Why?

_____

_____

_____

_____

_____

_____

_____

_____

_____

Chapter Six

REVIEWS AND OTHER EXPRESSIONS OF OPINION

Many commercial websites, including Amazon.com, Netflix.com, and Apple.com, encourage their users to write and post buyers' or users' reviews. Many of these sites even ask their users to review the reviewers by having them indicate whether a particular review was useful to them. Thus, clearly, at least one of the qualities of a good review is that it be useful.

But useful in what way? What, exactly, is a review?

In its simplest form, a review is a statement of the writer's opinion of whatever product he or she is reviewing. Someone thinking of purchasing a new iPod can go to the Apple site and read dozens (sometimes hundreds) of reviews from people who have purchased that same iPod. What do these reviewers like about the product? What are its strengths? What did they dislike; what are its weaknesses?

Notice that even the title indicates the tone of the review. The writer clearly did not find this production astounding.

MEDIUM WOMEN: A REVIEW OF A MUSICAL VERSION OF LITTLE WOMEN
BY BILL MCMAHON

Let's face it, none of them are exactly little.

Except for Amy, and she's just plain creepy. Kind of like a Louisa May Alcott bobble-head.

Actress Sutton Foster was nominated for the 2005 Tony Award for Best Actress in a Musical for her portrayal of Jo in this production.

In fact, most of these girls are plainly thirty. But you have to give Sutton Foster credit—she makes you believe she's an adolescent. And even if she pushes and sweats a bit, well, adolescents are prone to do that. Besides, she has some heavy lifting to do here. Some visible effort is more than understandable.

Notice the subtle joke here. McMahon is suggesting that Sutton "carried" the entire production.

There's nothing actually awful about this musical of *Little Women*. It's beautifully produced, has two major star performances, gorgeous sets and costumes and an actual acoustic orchestra.

Since a stage musical consists of the book, lyrics, and music, the author is saying that there is nothing in this play that does not need improvement.

In fact, there's nothing wrong with it that a better book, better lyrics and better music wouldn't cure. But then, when one of the original producers decides he wants to *be* the composer, buys out the original songwriting team and inserts his own talent into the project, well...the results are pretty much what you'd expect.

This is verifiable fact.

Understatement.

Granted, it's a whole lot more entertaining than *Dracula: the Musical*. But so is dental work.

And while nothing is painful or unendurably tedious, this is a long show. Nearly three hours worth. And those three hours fly by like, well... three hours. The audience feels it's aged along with the characters by the time we get to the final anthem.

> "Long" is an interpretation.
>
> "Three hours" is a fact.

While we're on that subject, could we once again have Broadway scores that contain actual songs rather than pop anthems? I know this is not a new thought, but it seems to bear repeating. Particularly since producers keep putting up shows that sound like second string Barry Manilow, but with less interesting lyrics. Of course Sutton works her money note overzealously—she's trying to make you ignore just how ordinary the words and music are. It's not her fault my mind still wandered during the songs.

> "Less interesting" is an opinion.

However, it's Maureen McGovern who provides the most impressive feat of magic onstage. Her performance gives the amazing impression of being effortless, while all the time she is anchoring every scene she's in. And when she gets a song, jump back. Second rate material does nothing to slow this woman down. (After all, she began her career in *The Poseidon Adventure,* warbling on a capsized ocean liner. You think poor writing can touch her? Guess again.) And while she can't convince you that what she's singing is actually good, she makes you believe that she thinks it is, and puts out accordingly. She makes her eleven-o'clock number so convincing, you can't help but cheer for her, and more importantly, the character. That's a pro.

> Actress and singer Maureen McGovern was nominated for the 2005 Drama Desk Award for Outstanding Featured Actress in a Musical for her portrayal of Marmee.

> This is a fact.
> "Warbling" expresses an opinion.

> A good, well-balanced review will evaluate the strengths of what is being reviewed as well as its weaknesses.

Both statements about "first rate talent" and "second rate material" are, of course, opinions.

Holding the producers responsible for what he believes is the decline of musical theater is McMahon's opinion.

She and Sutton both deserve a show equal to their talents. But how many times do we find ourselves saying that after spending a less than fulfilling evening on Broadway? Too often, of course. In fact, the one truly dispiriting thing about *Little Women* is the spectacle of so much first rate talent being lavished on such second rate material. If someone could just find a way to take the ego, self-delusion and deal-brokering mindset out of producing, we might actually get some projects worthy of these pros.

Of course, that seems about as likely as the father returning anytime soon in *Little Women*. We live through these girls' adolescence, growth, marriages and even the Civil War, and still no sign of Dad. Hmmmmm...

Maybe he's in Chattanooga. Living with a woman who's not so little.

In any case, girls, wake up. He ain't coming back.

January 27, 2005

EXERCISE ONE:

Answer the following questions about the review, "Medium Women." Be certain to base your answers on what the review actually says and not on your reaction—either positive or negative—to the review or the person who wrote it.

1. Given the tone and nature of this review, who would you say was Bill McMahon's intended audience? How do you know?

_____

_____

_____

_____

_____

_____

_____

_____

2. This is clearly an essentially negative review. What is the tone of McMahon's criticism?

_____

_____

_____

_____

_____

_____

_____

_____

3. List a few words or phrases McMahon uses to achieve this tone.

_____

_____

_____

_____

_____

_____

_____

_____

4. What are some of this play's chief shortcomings?

_____

_____

_____

_____

_____

_____

_____

5. What are some of its strengths?

_____

_____

_____

_____

_____

_____

_____

SPAMINATOR:
A REVIEW OF SPAMALOT:
THE MUSICAL
BY BILL MCMAHON

Well, I think René Magritte would have been amused. He might even have taken his brush up and inscribed "This is Not A Musical" on the proscenium in his perfect hand-painted letters.

René Magritte was a surrealist painter. One of his more famous paintings is of a tobacco pipe. Underneath are the words, "Ceci n'est pas une pipe," which means "This is not a pipe."

Okay, I'm totally aware that's a really *ponsy* reference, as the Pythons might say. But I'm trying hard to sum up my response to this year's Tony-Awarded Best Musical.

It's not that I didn't have a good time—not exactly. It's just that, more often than not, I felt like the one guest at the party who hadn't had enough cocktails. Perhaps this is the way some people feel at drag shows—lightly amused but somehow oddly removed.

And if you're thinking, "You're just not a *Monty Python* fan," well, you're right. Not in the sense that I didn't enjoy the original TV show—I did. But I'm not a fan in the fanatical sense, and there lies (part of) the rub. And I will say, having recently seen the source material, *Monty Python and the Holy Grail* (a homework assignment from our friends Denise and Brian) that I did find the show funnier than the movie, which admittedly left both of us scratching our heads last Tuesday when we ran the DVD. I'm aware the film has achieved a kind of uber-cult status among its legion of admirers, who are currently storming the box office of the Shubert Theatre, rapidly adding to what must be, by now, a $30 million advance.

I just have to confess—and I'm sorry, Pythonites—that in the larger sense, I just don't get it. Maybe it's me.

Let me just say, there is plenty to admire in *Spamalot*. Very talented people are doing some very funny things. In fact (and once again, I know I may be speaking sacrilege to some of you out there) the cast onstage is probably funnier than the original Pythons. These are, after all, top-of-the-line, seasoned pros, being directed by Mike Nichols, who damn well knows from funny. I particularly found David Hyde Pierce, Michael McGrath, Christopher Sieber and Alan Tudyk (the replacement for Hank Azaria) nearly as irresistible as I ultimately found the show itself resistible. And Sara Ramirez, to quote Hammerstein, "is broad where a broad should be broad." Plus there is some very adept lampooning of Broadway itself—in fact, the whole enterprise feels like a thumb in the eye to the current mindset of mainstream Broadway producing. Including some very well aimed barbs at Andrew Lloyd Webber, the lamentable pop-anthem tendency of certain scores ("The Song That Goes Like This", "Find Your Grail") and the whole "let's do an expensive adaptation of a title already pre-sold with the audience" phenomenon. On this level, I do get the joke.

Which is where my Magritte reference comes in.

The problem is, it gets kind of hard, after a certain point, to ignore the fact that *Spamalot* is, on a certain level, a pluperfect example of what it's sending up. As my partner said at intermission, it might well be funnier off-Broadway in a $150,000 production, than it is in an $11 million package on the stage of the Shubert. Things tend to get a little forced, even though the show is canny enough to make fun of its own bloat (some of the scenes take place in "A Very Expensive Forest"). And once you get the joke, well...you've gotten it, and you're waiting to move on. And as expertly as this fluff is served, something does get lost in the upscale translation, which is the sense of chaos that was always present in the original Python outings. The book is slavishly devoted to recreating the scenes from the movie that the audience is expecting (killer rabbit, Black Knight, all that). And the comedy lands—you don't get Mike Nichols to direct and not have the comedy land—but it feels as choreographed as a Susan Stroman number.

At the end of the night, the show is, while determinedly not self-reverential, decidedly self-*referential*. It exists in its own self-contained universe. You're either in the club or you're not. And while I found it refreshing to be at a behemoth production that for once was insisting on not taking itself seriously, at a certain point it begins to feel like a law of diminishing returns. At least for an outsider.

And if they start talking about *Airplane! the Musical*, well...

But don't get me going.

June 10, 2005

EXERCISE TWO:

Answer the following questions about the review, "Spaminator." Be certain to base your answers on what the letter actually says and not on your reaction—either positive or negative—to the review or the person who wrote it.

1. At what point does it become clear whether this is a positive or negative review?

_____

_____

_____

_____

_____

_____

_____

2. What are some facts McMahon cites in his review?

_____

_____

_____

_____

_____

_____

_____

3. What are some interpretations of fact?

_____

_____

_____

_____

_____

_____

4. What are some opinions?

_____

_____

_____

_____

_____

_____

_____

5. What does beginning with the Magritte allusion and then mentioning it again later contribute to the tone of the review?

_____

_____

_____

_____

_____

_____

_____

6. What, according to McMahon, are some of this play's chief shortcomings?

_____

_____

_____

_____

_____

_____

_____

7. What are some of its strengths?

_____

_____

_____

_____

_____

_____

_____

Writing Opportunity One: Choose one book, play, movie, television program, audio CD, or video game that you like and one that you don't. Write a brief but well-balanced review of each.

SCIENCE AND RELIGION: AN EVOLUTION SUNDAY SERMON, MARCH 2, 2008
BY REV. SCOTTY MCLENNAN

Is there any way to reconcile science and religion? That's my sermon topic today. In our scripture readings we have the Genesis creation story to deal with,[1] along with Matthew's gospel account of Jesus being tempted by the devil to defy the law of gravity by throwing himself off the pinnacle of the temple in Jerusalem.[2] What do we do with the Biblical claim that the universe as we know it—including the earth with vegetation, living creatures of every kind and human beings—was all created in six days? What would really have happened if Jesus had thrown himself off the temple, rather than wisely responding "Do not put the Lord your God to the test"?[3]

Journalist Christopher Hitchens was on campus a month ago. As many of you know, he's the author of a current best-seller entitled *God is Not Great: How Religion Poisons Everything.*[4] In the first chapter of that book he states one of his irreducible objections to religious faith: "It wholly misrepresents the origins of man and the cosmos."[5] He explains that he "distrust[s] anything that contradicts science or outrages reason."[6] One of the major problems for religion is that it "comes from the period of human prehistory where nobody … had the smallest idea of what was going on. It comes from the bawling and fearful infancy of our species, and is a babyish attempt to meet our

Some may argue that the sermon portion of a worship service is essentially persuasive, but McLennan presents this sermon more as a reflection for his congregation to consider than an argument with which he hopes they'll agree.

McLennan is addressing a very specific audience, essentially students and faculty of Stanford University in California.

inescapable need for knowledge ... Today the least educated of my children knows much more about the natural order than any of the founders of religion ... All attempts to reconcile faith with science and reason are consigned to failure and ridicule for precisely these reasons."[7]

By contrast, the late Rev. Jerry Falwell, founder of Liberty University in Lynchburg Virginia—a university which now has more than 20,000 students[8]—wrote that "The Bible is the inerrant ... word of the living God. It is absolutely infallible, without error in all matters pertaining to faith and practice, as well as in areas such as geography, science, history, etc."[9] Last year the *New York Times* published an article about a professor of earth sciences at Liberty University, Marcus Ross, who received his Ph.D. in geosciences from the University of Rhode Island. He believes that the Bible presents a literally true account of the creation of the universe, and that the earth is at most 10,000 years old.[10]

By citing Hitchens, Falwell, and Ross, McLennan achieves balance. As he has not spoken in support of either view, he cannot yet be charged with bias—or even of expressing an opinion.

Today at the Stanford Memorial Church we're celebrating "Evolution Sunday." We're part of a national movement, as you'll see in the note in the announcements section of the order of service, of more than 535 congregations across the country and around the world, committed to affirming that timeless religious truths and the discoveries of modern science can comfortably coexist. Associate Dean Joanne Sanders and I are among more than 10,000 Christian clergy who have signed an open letter which states, in part, that the majority of Christians don't read the Bible literally, as they would a science textbook, and that many of the beloved stories found in the Bible, such as the Genesis account of creation (as

Here he identifies an argument—a thesis.

read this morning)[11] convey truths of a different
order than scientific truth. They touch hearts,
as is the province of great literature, poetry, and
art, but they are not intended to convey scientific
information. Here's where both Hitchens and
Falwell are wrong. I quote from the letter
now: "We believe that the theory of evolution
is a foundational scientific truth, one that has
stood up to rigorous scrutiny and upon which
much of human knowledge and achievement
rests. To reject this truth or to treat it as 'one
theory among others' is to deliberately embrace
scientific ignorance and transmit such ignorance
to our children. We believe that among God's
good gifts are human minds capable of critical
thought … We ask that science remain science
and that religion remain religion, two very
different, but complementary, forms of truth."

This has been a good quarter at Stanford to
explore the relationship of science and religion,
because we also had physician-geneticist Francis
Collins, Director of the National Human Genome
Research Institute, on campus last month. He
directs the multinational 2,400-scientist team
that mapped the 3 billion letters of the human
DNA blueprint. He is also a devout Christian
who converted from atheism at the age of 27
and now advises evangelical scientists on how to
reconcile their faith with their scientific careers.[12]
He's a best-selling author himself, having written
The Language of God, which came out in 2006.

In his Stanford talk on "God and the Genome" to
an overflow audience in Memorial Auditorium
on February 5, Collins asserted that science and
religion tend to address different questions: how
versus why. Science discovers natural laws, which

tell us how the universe operates. Religion asks big existential questions like "Why is there something instead of nothing?" But there are also ways in which religion and science overlap, of necessity. Collins says that his faith must rest squarely upon what he knows through logic and reason and science. Skepticism and doubt, of the sort encouraged by the scientific method, are critical to the development and testing of faith. Evolution is a scientific theory like gravity, which has been proven beyond a shadow of a doubt. Biblical literalism is a major problem when it leads to results like seeing the universe as we now know it having been created in six days, or human beings as having been created out of the blue, just as we now are, rather than having evolved from other living organisms which first appeared on the earth billions of years ago; our own species, homo sapiens, evolved from primate ancestors about 200,000 years ago.[13]

Collins calls himself a theistic evolutionist. For him DNA is the way God spoke life into being, and evolution is the mechanism by which God's plan has been carried out. One might ask, though, why do you need God at all? Why aren't the scientific answers alone enough? My personal answer traces back to a course I took in my freshman year on human evolution from a geneticist and evolutionary biologist named Theodosius Dobzhansky. He cited the great Russian novelist Dostoevsky as having said that "Man needs the unfathomable and the infinite just as much as he does the small planet which he inhabits."[14] Then, Dobzhansky pointed out how Darwin himself had assumed a Creator God behind all those natural laws like gravity and natural selection that have continued to work consistently and reliably throughout the ages.

Notice again that, while it is clear on which side of the controversy McLennan falls, he is representing his beliefs alone, not speaking to convince his audience to agree with him.

In Darwin's revolutionary book, *On the Origin of Species*, he declared:

> To my mind it accords better with what we know of the laws impressed on matter by the Creator, that ... [we] view all beings not as special creations, but as the lineal descendants of some few beings which lived long before the first bed of the Silurian system was deposited...

> It is interesting to contemplate an entangled bank, clothed with many plants of many kinds, with birds singing on the bushes, with various insects flitting about, and with worms crawling through the damp earth, and to reflect that these elaborately constructed forms, so different from each other, and dependent on each other in so complex a manner, have all been produced by laws acting around us ... There is grandeur in this view of life ... having been originally breathed into a few forms or into one; and that, whilst this planet has gone cycling on according to the fixed law of gravity, from so simple a beginning, endless forms most beautiful and most wonderful have been, and are being, evolved.[15]

There's another way in which Francis Collins references God. He talks about the improbability of life, and especially of human life, as having occurred just by chance. Several scientific constants were necessary. Gravitation was one of them, and if it had been off by just "one part in a hundred million million, then the expansion of the universe after the Big Bang would not have occurred in the fashion that was necessary for life to occur." A designer becomes "a rather plausible explanation for what is otherwise an exceedingly improbable event—namely, our existence." Collins recognizes that other scientific theories have been proposed, like our universe being only one of a very large number of parallel universes, so the odds would then increase that a tiny minority of universes, like ours, will have just the right fine-tuning to support life somewhere within them. But Collins finds the explanation of a creator God to be more compelling in its simplicity and elegance than "the bubbling of all these multiverses."[16]

However, he disagrees with the modern proponents of so-called "Intelligent Design" (capital I, capital D), a theory first propounded by a Cal-Berkeley law professor in 1991.[17] Advocates of Intelligent Design challenge the theory of evolution by claiming that there are cases of irreducible complexity, like the human eye or the blood clotting mechanism, which could not have occurred stepwise through the long process of evolutionary natural selection. Instead, an intelligent designer must have stepped in and created these particular organs and functions, full-blown in all of their complexity, in one fell swoop. Collins retorts that these arguments have no scientific merit, and each of the claims that particular mechanisms could not have evolved through step-by-step natural selection have since been refuted.[18] There are also important theological objections to Intelligent Design theory, since it reduces God to certain gaps in current scientific explanation; God will be whittled away even more as those gaps are filled in scientifically in the future, as they have been in the past. Also, Intelligent Design theory ends up portraying God "as a clumsy Creator, having to intervene

Notice that McLennan is going to devote some time to explaining the predominant opposing view.

at regular intervals to fix the inadequacies of
his own initial plan," which supposedly had
included trustworthy, consistent natural laws.[19]
In summary, Collins finds Intelligent Design to be
simultaneously bad science and bad theology.

A week from today evolutionary biologist
Richard Dawkins will be on campus. He's
written another best-selling book called *The
God Delusion*.[20] Just over a year ago there was
a cover story in *Time* Magazine entitled "God
vs. Science,"[21] which featured a debate between
Dawkins and Collins. Collins suggests that
atheists like Dawkins "sometimes come across
as a bit arrogant … characterizing faith as
something only an idiot would attach themselves
to."[22] Dawkins suggests that Christians like
Collins should realize from the discoveries
of modern science that "If there is a God, it's
going to be a whole lot bigger and a whole lot
more incomprehensible than anything that any
theologian of any religion has ever proposed."[23]

One area where the two of them seem to
agree, however, is in resisting the attempts of
the religious right and the federal government
to denigrate or curtail modern science. Both
scientists are in favor of opening new stem-cell
lines to develop medical cures and save lives. They
are both concerned about good science education
in our schools, from kindergarten all the way
through graduate and medical school. This is an
area that the 10,000 signatories of the clergy letter
for Evolution Sunday are also deeply concerned
about: "We urge school board members to
preserve the integrity of the science curriculum by
affirming the teaching of the theory of evolution
as a core component of human knowledge."

It's astounding to realize that in a 2004 Gallup poll, 45% of Americans chose this statement, when asked which of three came closest to their views on the origin and developments of human beings: "God created human beings pretty much in their present form at one time within the last 10,000 years or so."[24] Stanford professor of evolutionary biology Joan Roughgarden, in a little book called *Evolution and Christian Faith*, where she reconciles science and religion for herself, cites another 2004 poll which found that 35% of Protestant doctors believe that "God created humans exactly as they appear now." These are American physicians who have made it all the way through college and medical school and are now practicing medicine! 65% of all physicians approve of teaching biblical creationism alongside evolution in our public schools. Perhaps this wouldn't be utterly worrisome, if polls didn't also show that 40% of Americans want to replace evolution with creationism in our public school science curriculum.[25]

There's too much that really matters in our world than to allow conservative religion to trump science education about evolution, starting with medical cures based on the genome project and stem-cell research. There are implications for our economy as well—will we not train our children to be scientifically competitive in the global marketplace? There are implications for understanding our environment and ultimately for saving the earth.

It's time now for a reconciliation between science and religion that allows both to flourish and to complement each other. Francis Collins at the end of his book calls for "a truce in the escalating war between science and spirit." He claims that

"Like so many earthly wars, this one has been initiated and intensified by extremists on both sides, sounding alarms that predict imminent ruin unless the other side is vanquished ... Abandon the battlements. Our hopes, joys, and the future of our world depend on it."[26]

The Reverend William L. "Scotty" McLennan, Jr. is the Dean of Religious Life at Stanford University and one of the models for the character of "Reverend Scot Sloan" in the satiric comic strip, Doonesbury.

1 Genesis 1:24—2:4.

2 Matthew 4:1-10.

3 Matthew 4:7.

4 Christopher Hitchens, God is Not Great: How Religion Poisons Everything (New York: Twelve, 2007).

5 Hitchens, God is Not Great, p. 4.

6 Hitchens, God is Not Great, p. 5.

7 Hitchens, God is Not Great, p. 64-65.

8 "Admissions," Liberty University, http://www.liberty.edu/admissions

9 Jerry Falwell, Listen, America! (New York: Bantam, 1981). (As quoted in John C. Bennett, "Assessing the Concerns of the Religious Right," Christian Century, October 14, 1981, pp. 1018-1022).

10 Cornelia Dean, "Believing Scripture but Playing by Science's Rules," New York Times (February 12, 2007).

11 Genesis 1:24—2:4.

12 David Van Biema, "God vs. Science," Time (November 2, 2006).

13 Francis S. Collins, The Language of God (New York: Free Press, 2006), pp. 89, 96.

14 Theodosius Dobzhansky, The Biology of Ultimate Concern (New York: New American Library, 1967), p. 63

15 Charles Darwin, On the Origin of Species by Means of Natural Selection, or the Preservation of Favoured Races in the Struggle for Life (London: John Murray, 1859).

16 Van Biema, "God vs. Science."

17 Phillip E. Johnson, Darwin on Trial (Regnery Gateway, Washington, DC, 1991).

18 Collins, The Language of God, pp. 186-193.

19 Collins, The Language of God, pp. 193-194.

20 Richard Dawkins, The God Delusion (Boston: Houghton Mifflin Company, 2006).

21 David Van Biema, "God vs. Science," Time (November 2, 2006).

22 Biema, "God vs. Science."

23 Biema, "God vs. Science."

24 Collins, The Language of God, p. 147.

25 Joan Roughgarden, Evolution and Christian Faith (Washington: Island Press, 2006).

26 Collins, The Language of God, pp. 233-234.

EXERCISE THREE:

Answer the following questions about Reverend "Scotty" McLennan's sermon, "Science and Religion." Be certain to base your answers on what the sermon actually says and not on your reaction—either positive or negative—to the sermon or the person who wrote it.

1. Is the letter to which McLennan refers when he says, "Associate Dean Joanne Sanders and I ... have signed an open letter which states ..." founded in fact, analysis, interpretation, or opinion? How do you know?

_____

_____

_____

_____

_____

2. Is McLennan's quoting from the letter intended to be persuasive or informative? How do you know?

_____

_____

_____

_____

_____

3. What is McLennan's most likely purpose for mentioning Francis Collins and his earlier visit to the campus?

_____

_____

_____

_____

_____

4. Are McLennan's claims about Francis Collins facts or opinion?

_____

_____

_____

_____

_____

_____

5. List and identify some logical fallacies (if any) that McLennan uses in this sermon.

_____

_____

_____

_____

_____

6. List and identify some techniques of propaganda (if any) that McLennan uses in this sermon.

_____

_____

_____

_____

_____

Chapter Seven
MEMOIRS AND PERSONAL ESSAYS

If you've ever read someone's blog or "friended" someone on Internet social sites like Facebook or Myspace, you know that people enjoy writing about themselves—recording their thoughts and feelings or reporting on daily events—and they enjoy hearing about others' lives. This is not a new phenomenon, and much nonfiction literature takes the form of memoirs, personal letters, journals and diaries, and other personal accounts. Generally, the reader of these forms expects a certain amount of slant or even bias, since the basis of the personal essay is centered on the writer's own impressions, rather than the reader's reaction.

Consider the following pieces, both expressing some degree of emotion on the part of the writer. The first is a poignant account by *Frankenstein* author Mary Shelley on the drowning death of her husband, poet Percy Bysshe Shelley. The second is a tongue-in-cheek anecdote from an author's life.

MRS. SHELLEY TO MRS. [MARIA] GISBORNE
BY MARY SHELLEY

August 1822.

I said in a letter to Peacock[1], my dear Mrs. Gisborne, that I would send you some account of the last miserable months of my disastrous life. From day to day I have put this off, but I will now endeavor to fulfill my design. The scene of my existence is closed, and though there be no pleasure in retracing the scenes that have preceded the event which has crushed my hopes, yet there seems to be a necessity in doing so, and I obey the impulse that urges me. I wrote to you either at the end of May or the beginning of June. I described to you the place we were living in our desolate house, the beauty yet strangeness of the scenery, and the delight Shelley took in all this. He never was in better health or spirits than during this time. I was not well in body or mind. My nerves were wound up to the utmost irritation, and the sense of misfortune hung over my spirits.

No words can tell you how I hated our house and the country about it. Shelley reproached me for this. His health was good, and the place was quite after his own heart. What could I answer? That the people were wild and hateful, that though the country was beautiful, yet I

Notice the highly emotional language. In this use, it is not propaganda, as Shelley is describing her feelings. She is not claiming to be offering an objective account or trying to argue a point.

---

1 Thomas Love Peacock (1785–1866) was a British satirist and a close friend of the Shelleys.

liked a more countrified place, that there was great difficulty in living, that all our Tuscans would leave us, and that the very jargon of these *Genovesi* was disgusting. This was all I had to say, but no words could describe my feelings; the beauty of the woods made me weep and shudder; so vehement was my feeling of dislike that I used to rejoice when the winds and waves permitted me to go out in the boat, so that I was not obliged to take my usual walk among the shaded paths, alleys of vine festooned trees all that before I doted on, and that now weighed on me. My only moments of peace were on board that unhappy boat when, lying down with my head on his knee, I shut my eyes and felt the wind and our swift motion alone. My ill health might account for much of this.

Bathing in the sea somewhat relieved me, but on the 8th of June (I think it was) I was threatened with a miscarriage[1], and after a week of great ill health, on Sunday, the 16th, this took place at 8 in the morning. I was so ill that for seven hours I lay nearly lifeless kept from fainting by brandy, vinegar, and *eau-de-Cologne*, etc. At length ice was brought to our solitude; it came before the doctor, so Claire[2] and Jane[3] were afraid of using it, but Shelley overruled them, and by an unsparing application of it I was restored. They all thought, and so did I at one time, that I was about to die, I hardly wished that I had; my own Shelley could never have lived without me; the

---

1 Mary Shelley had already experienced the deaths of three children. Only her son Percy Florence (1819–1889) survived childhood.

2 Claire Clairmont, Mary Shelley's stepsister and an occasional lover of Lord Byron.

3 Jane Williams, wife of Edward Williams, a Bengal army officer and friend of Percy Shelley, who died with Shelley on 8 July 1822.

sense of eternal misfortune would have pressed too heavily upon him, and what would have become of my poor babe? My convalescence was slow, and during it a strange occurrence happened to retard it. But first I must describe our house to you. The floor on which we lived was thus:

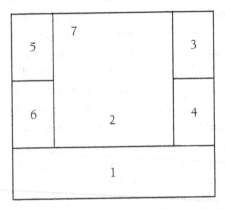

1 is a terrace that went the whole length of our house and was precipitous to the sea; 2, the large dining-hall; 3, a private staircase; 4, my bedroom; 5, Mrs. Williams' bedroom; 6, Shelley's; and 7, the entrance from the great staircase. Now to return. As I said, Shelley was at first in perfect health, but having over-fatigued himself one day, and then the fright my illness gave him, caused a return of nervous sensations and visions as bad as in his worst times. I think it was the Saturday after my illness, while yet unable to walk, I was confined to my bed in the middle of the night I was awoke by hearing him scream and come rushing into my room; I was sure that he was asleep, and tried to waken him by calling on him, but he continued to scream, which inspired me with such a panic that I jumped out of bed and ran across the hall to Mrs. Williams' room, where I fell through weakness, though I was so frightened that I got up again immediately.

She let me in, and Williams went to Shelley, who had been wakened by my getting out of bed. He said that he had not been asleep, and that it was a vision that he saw that had frightened him. But as he declared that he had not screamed, it was certainly a dream, and no waking vision. What had frightened him was this. He dreamt that, lying as he did in bed, Edward and Jane [Williams] came in to him; they were in the most horrible condition; their bodies lacerated, their bones starting through their skin, their faces pale yet stained with blood; they could hardly walk, but Edward was the weakest, and Jane was supporting him. Edward said, "Get up, Shelley, the sea is flooding the house, and it is all coming down."

Shelley got up, he thought, and went to his window that looked on the terrace and the sea, and thought he saw the sea rushing in. Suddenly his vision changed, and he saw the figure of himself strangling me; that had made him rush into my room, yet, fearful of frightening me, he dared not approach the bed, when my jumping out awoke him, or, as he phrased it, caused his vision to vanish. All this was frightful enough, and talking it over the next morning, he told me that he had had many visions lately; he had seen the figure of himself, which met him as he walked on the terrace and said to him, "How long do you mean to be content?" no very terrific words, and certainly not prophetic of what has occurred. But Shelley had often seen these figures when ill; but the strangest thing is that Mrs. Williams saw him. Now Jane, though a woman of sensibility, has not much imagination, and is not in the slightest degree nervous, neither in dreams nor otherwise. She was standing one day, the day before I was taken ill, at a window that looked on the terrace, with Trelawny[1]. It was day. She saw, as she thought, Shelley pass by the window, as he often was then, without a coat or jacket; he passed again. Now, as he passed both times the same way, and as from the side towards which he went each time there was no way to get back except past the window again (except over a wall 20 feet from the ground), she was struck at her seeing him pass twice thus, and looked out and seeing him no more, she cried, "Good God, can Shelley have leapt from the wall? Where can he be gone?"

"Shelley," said Trelawny, "no Shelley has passed. What do you mean?" Trelawny says that she trembled exceedingly when she heard this, and it proved, indeed, that Shelley had never been on the terrace, and was far off at the time she saw him. Well, we thought no more of these things, and I slowly got better. Having heard from Hunt[2] that he had sailed from Genoa, on Monday, 1st July, Shelley, Edward [Williams], and Captain Roberts (the gentleman who built our boat) departed in our boat for Leghorn[3] to receive him.

I was then just better, had begun to crawl from my bedroom to the terrace, but bad spirits succeeded to ill health, and this departure of Shelley's seemed to add insufferably to my misery. I could not endure that he should go. I called him back two or three times, and told him that if I did not see him soon I would go to Pisa with the child. I cried bitterly when he went away. They went, and Jane, Clare, and I remained alone with the children. I could not walk out,

---

1 *Edward Trewlany (1792–1881); an English novelist and adventurer.*

2 *Leigh Hunt (1784 – 1859); an English critic, essayist, and poet.*

3 *The Italian city of Livorno.*

and though I gradually gathered strength, it was slowly, and my ill spirits increased. In my letters to him I entreated him to return; "the feeling that some misfortune would happen," I said, "haunted me." I feared for the child, for the idea of danger connected with him never struck me. When Jane and Clare took their evening walk, I used to patrol the terrace, oppressed with wretchedness, yet gazing on the most beautiful scene in the world.

This Gulf of Spezzia is subdivided into many small bays, of which ours was far the most beautiful. The two horns of the bay (so to express myself) were wood-covered promontories, crowned with castles; at the foot of these, on the farthest, was *Lerici*, on the nearest *San Terenzo*; *Lerici* being above a mile by land from us, and *San Terenzo* about a hundred or two yards. Trees covered the hills that enclosed this bay, and their beautiful groups were picturesquely contrasted with the rocks, the castle, and the town. The sea lay far extended in front, while to the west we saw the promontory and islands, which formed one of the extreme boundaries of the Gulf. To see the sun set upon this scene, the stars shine, and the moon rise, was a sight of wondrous beauty, but to me it added only to my wretchedness. I repeated to myself all that another would have said to console me, and told myself the tale of love, peace, and competence which I enjoyed; but I answered myself by tears: Did not my William die, and did I hold my Percy[1] by a firmer tenure? Yet I thought when he, when my Shelley, returns, I shall be

---

1 *Shelley's first child, a daughter born prematurely, died in 1815. Her second child, William "Willmouse" Shelley, died of malaria in 1819. Of all the children Mary would have, only Percy Florence would survive childhood.*

happy; he will comfort me, if my boy be ill he will restore him, and encourage me. I had a letter or two from Shelley, mentioning the difficulties he had in establishing the Hunts, and that he was unable to fix the time of his return. Thus a week passed. On Monday, 8th, Jane had a letter from Edward, dated Saturday; he said that he waited at Leghorn for Shelley, who was at Pisa; that Shelley's return was certain; "but," he continued, "if he should not come by Monday, I will come in *a felucca*," and you may expect me Tuesday evening at farthest.

We have finally left the long passage of exposition and begun the focal event of the letter.

This was Monday, the fatal Monday, but with us it was stormy all day, and we did not at all suppose that they could put to sea. At 12 at night we had a thunderstorm; Tuesday it rained all day, and was calm. The sky wept on their graves. On Wednesday the wind was fair from Leghorn, and in the evening several *feluccas* arrived thence; one brought word that they had sailed on Monday, but we did not believe them.

Thursday was another day of fair wind, and when 12 at night came, and we did not see the tall sails of the little boat double the promontory before us, we began to fear, not the truth, but some illness, some disagreeable news for their detention. Jane got so uneasy that she determined to proceed the next day to Leghorn in a boat, to see what was the matter. Friday came, and with it a heavy sea and bad wind. Jane, however, resolved to be rowed to Leghorn (since no boat could sail), and busied herself in preparations. I wished her to wait for letters, since Friday was letter day. She would not; but the sea detained her; the swell rose so that no boat could venture out. At 12 at noon our letters came; there was one from Hunt to Shelley; it said, "Pray write to tell us how you got home, for they say that you had bad weather after you sailed Monday, and we are anxious." The paper fell from me. I trembled all over. Jane read it.

"Then it is all over," she said.

"No, my dear Jane," I cried, "it is not all over, but this suspense is dreadful. Come with me, we will go to Leghorn; we will post to be swift, and learn our fate." We crossed to *Lerici*, despair in our hearts; they raised our spirits there by telling us that no accident had been heard of, and that it must have been known, etc., but still our fear was great, and without resting we posted to Pisa. It must have been fearful to see us two poor, wild, aghast creatures driving (like Matilda) towards the sea, to learn if we were to be for ever doomed to misery. I knew that Hunt was at Pisa, at Lord Byron's house, but I thought that Lord Byron was at Leghorn. I settled that we should drive to *Casa Lanfranchi*, that I should get out, and ask the fearful question of Hunt, "Do you know anything of Shelley?" On entering Pisa, the idea of seeing Hunt for the first time for four years, under such circumstances, and asking him such a question, was so terrific to me, that it was with difficulty that I prevented myself from going into convulsions. My struggles were dreadful. They knocked at the door, and some one called out, *chi e*. It was the Guiccioli's maid. Lord Byron was in Pisa. Hunt was in bed; so I was to see Lord Byron instead of him. This was a great relief to me.

I staggered upstairs; the Guiccioli came to meet me, smiling, while I could hardly say, "Where is he—*Sapete alcuna cosa di Shelley*?"

> Although the reader knows the history of Percy Shelley's death, Mary Shelley achieves suspense in her narrating the events.

> Shelley is alluding to her own second novel.

213

They knew nothing; he had left Pisa on Sunday; on Monday he had sailed; there had been bad weather Monday afternoon. More they knew not. Both Lord Byron and the lady have told me since, that on that terrific evening I looked more like a ghost than a woman. Light seemed to emanate from my features; my face was very white; I looked like marble. Alas! I had risen almost from a bed of sickness for this journey; I had traveled all day; it was now 12 at night, and we, refusing to rest, proceeded to Leghorn—not in despair no, for then we must have died; but with sufficient hope to keep up the agitation of the spirits, which was all my life.

It was past 2 in the morning when we arrived. They took us to the wrong inn; neither Trelawny nor Captain Roberts were there, nor did we exactly know where they were, so we were obliged to wait until daylight: we threw ourselves, dressed, on our beds and slept a little, but at 6 o'clock we went to one or two inns, to ask for one or the other of these gentlemen. We found Roberts at the "Globe." He came down to us with a face that seemed to tell us that the worst was true, and here we learned all that occurred during the week they had been absent from us, and under what circumstances they had departed on their return.

Shelley had passed most of the time at Pisa, arranging the affairs of the Hunts, and screwing Lord Byron's mind to the sticking place about the journal. He had found this a difficult task at first, but at length he had succeeded to his heart's content with both points. Mrs. Mason said that she saw him in better health and spirits than she had ever known him, when he took leave of her,

Sunday, July 7, his face burnt by the sun, and his heart light, that he had succeeded in rendering the Hunts tolerably comfortable. Edward had remained at Leghorn.

On Monday, July 8, during the morning, they were employed in buying many things, eatables, etc., for our solitude. There had been a thunderstorm early, but about noon the weather was fine, and the wind right fair for *Lerici*. They were impatient to be gone. Roberts said, "Stay until tomorrow, to see if the weather is settled;" and Shelley might have stayed, but Edward was in so great an anxiety to reach home, saying they would get there in seven hours with that wind, that they sailed; Shelley being in one of those extravagant fits of good spirits, in which you have sometimes seen him. Roberts went out to the end of the mole, and watched them out of sight; they sailed at 1, and went off at the rate of about seven knots. About 3, Roberts, who was still on the mole, saw wind coming from the Gulf, or rather what the Italians call *a temporale*. Anxious to know how the boat would weather the storm, he got leave to go up the tower, and, with the glass, discovered them about ten miles out at sea, off *Via Reggio*; they were taking in their topsails. "The haze of the storm," he said, "hid them from me, and I saw them no more. When the storm cleared, I looked again, fancying that I should see them on their return to us, but there was no boat on the sea."

This, then, was all we knew, yet we did not despair; they might have been driven over to Corsica, and not knowing the coast, have gone God knows where. Reports favored this belief; it was even said that they had been seen in the Gulf. We resolved to return with all possible speed; we sent a courier to go from tower to tower, along the coast, to know if anything had been seen or found, and at 9 A.M. we quitted Leghorn, stopped but one moment at Pisa, and proceeded towards *Lerici*. When at two miles from *Via Reggio*, we rode down to that town to know if they knew anything.

Here our calamity first began to break on us; a little boat and a water cask had been found five miles off. They had manufactured a *piccolissima lancia* of thin planks stitched by a shoemaker, just to let them run on shore without wetting themselves, as our boat drew four feet of water. The description of that found tallied with this, but then this boat was very cumbersome, and in bad weather they might have been easily led to throw it overboard, the cask frightened me most, but the same reason might in some sort be given for that. I must tell you that Jane and I were not now alone.

Trelawny accompanied us back to our home. We journeyed on and reached the *Magra* about half-past 10 P.M. I cannot describe to you what I felt in the first moment when, fording this river, I felt the water splash about our wheels. I was suffocated; I gasped for breath; I thought I should have gone into convulsions, and I struggled violently that Jane might not perceive it. Looking down the river I saw the two great lights burning at the face; a voice from within me seemed to cry aloud, "That is his grave."

After passing the river, I gradually recovered. Arriving at *Lerici*, we were obliged to cross our little bay in a boat. San Arenzo was illuminated for a *festa*. What a scene! The waving sea, the

sirocco wind, the lights of the town towards
which we rowed, and our own desolate hearts,
that colored all with a shroud. We landed.

Nothing had been heard of them.

This was Saturday, July 13, and thus we waited
until Thursday July 18, thrown about by hope
and fear. We sent messengers along the coast
towards Genoa and to *Via Reggio*; nothing had
been found more than the *Lancetta*; reports were
brought us; we hoped; and yet to tell you all the
agony we endured during those twelve days,
would be to make you conceive a universe of pain
each moment intolerable, and giving place to one
still worse. The people of the country, too, added
to one's discomfort; they are like wild savages;
on *festas*, the men and women and children in
different bands—the sexes always separate—pass
the whole night in dancing on the sands close to
our door; running into the sea, then back again,
and screaming all the time one perpetual air, the
most detestable in the world; then the sirocco
perpetually blew, and the sea for ever moaned
their dirge. On Thursday, 18th, Trelawny left us
to go to Leghorn, to see what was doing or what
could be done. On Friday I was very ill; but as
evening came on, I said to Jane, "If anything had
been found on the coast, Trelawny would have
returned to let us know. He has not returned, so
I hope." About 7 o'clock P.M. he did return; all
was over, all was quiet now; they had been found
washed on shore. Well, all this was to be endured.

Well, what more have I to say? The next day we
returned to Pisa, and here we are still. Days pass
away, one after another, and we live thus; we
are all together; we shall quit Italy together. Jane

must proceed to London. If letters do not alter my views, I shall remain in Paris. Thus we live, seeing the Hunts now and then. Poor Hunt has suffered terribly, as you may guess. Lord Byron is very kind to me, and comes with the Guiccioli to see me often. Today, this day, the sun shining in the sky, they are gone to the desolate sea-coast to perform the last offices to their earthly remains, Hunt, Lord Byron, and Trelawny. The quarantine laws would not permit us to remove them sooner, and now only on condition that we burn them to ashes.

That I do not dislike. His rest shall be at Rome beside my child, where one day I also shall join them. *Adonais*[1] is not Keats', it is his own elegy; he bids you there go to Rome. I have seen the spot where he now lies, the sticks that mark the spot where the sands cover him; he shall not be there, it is too near *Via Reggio*. They are now about this fearful office, and I live!

One more circumstance I will mention. As I said, he took leave of Mrs. Mason in high spirits on Sunday.

"Never," said she, "did I see him look happier than the last glance I had of his countenance." On Monday he was lost. On Monday night she dreamt that she was somewhere, she knew not where, and he came, looking very pale and fearfully melancholy. She said to him, "You look ill; you are tired; sit down and eat."

"No," he replied, "I shall never eat more; I have not a *soldo* left in the world."

---

1 Adonais *is an elegy written by Percy Shelly in 1821 on the death of poet John Keats.*

"Nonsense," said she, "this is no inn, you need not pay."

"Perhaps," he answered, "it is the worse for that."

Then she awoke; and, going to sleep again, she dreamt that my Percy was dead; and she awoke crying bitterly so bitterly, and felt so miserable that she said to herself, "Why, if the little boy should die, I should not feel it in this manner."

She was so struck with these dreams, that she mentioned them to her servant the next day, saying she hoped all was well with us.

Well, here is my story the last story I shall have to tell.

All that might have been bright in my life is now despoiled. I shall live to improve myself, to take care of my child, and render myself worthy to join him. Soon my weary pilgrimage will begin. I rest now, but soon I must leave Italy, and then there is an end of all but despair. Adieu! I hope you are well and happy. I have an idea that while he was at Pisa, he received a letter from you that I have never seen; so not knowing where to direct, I shall send this letter to Peacock. I shall send it open; he may be glad to read it.

Yours ever truly, MARY W. S.

Mary Wollstonecraft Shelley (1797–1851) was the author of Frankenstein *and wife of Romantic poet Percy Bysshe Shelley.*

EXERCISE ONE:

Answer the following questions about Mary Shelley's letter to Maria Gisborne.
Be certain to base your answers on what the letter actually says and not on your
reaction—either positive or negative—to the letter or to Mary Shelley.

1. Remembering that Mary Shelley is writing this letter months after the event
   and admittedly after considerable thought and procrastination, how does she
   preface her description of Shelley's death?

   _____

   _____

   _____

   _____

   _____

   _____

   _____

   _____

2. What effect does Shelley's long passage of exposition—the background
   of Percy's vision, the description of the Gulf of Spezzia, etc.—have on the
   emotional impact of her letter? Why does she include it?

   _____

   _____

   _____

   _____

   _____

   _____

   _____

   _____

3. How does the tone of the letter change once Shelley completes her passage of exposition and returns to the narrative of her husband's death? What signals this change?

_____

_____

_____

_____

_____

_____

_____

4. What does Shelley's claim that this letter is "the last story I shall have to tell" reveal about the way she wrote this letter?

_____

_____

_____

_____

_____

_____

_____

Surviving the Author Photo
by Matthew Pearl

Saturday, August 22, 2009 at 2:34pm

Do you like having your photo taken?

As this is a casual, informal piece—a blog post—Pearl immediately establishes rapport with his reader.

I've always hated being in photos. For one phase of my teenage years most photos show me shielding my face from the camera. Maybe that's why I always like mafia movies, I could relate to their dislike of having their photos taken.

Hyperbole is a common technique for creating humor.

I hadn't considered the dreaded Author Photo until I was asked for one as we neared completion on *The Dante Club*. The publisher will sometimes ask you to try to take your own first, maybe by a member of your family.

I did a session with my dad. Did I ever tell you he was a photographer in his college years? He took photos of rockers like The Rolling Stones and Jimi Hendrix when they were first getting started. Later, he lost the negatives and most of the photos.

But he kept asking me to smile, which is what I most hated to do in photos. This is sort of a compromise between a smile and a sneer.

Photo credit: Warren Pearl. Copyright © 2003.

We took a few dozen of these in Mount Auburn Cemetery, Cambridge, where some scenes in the novel took place. For some reason it looks like I write political thrillers.

The publisher thought I looked too young. Well, I was 26, and have always looked younger than I am. When I was five, I guess I looked three.

So they sent me to a professional portrait photographer in New York named Beth Kelly. She was used to photographing actors and models who knew how to pose. She had never done an author photo. Poor woman!

I'm also not much of a clotheshorse, and needed help with my wardrobe. I brought two button-down shirts that were identical except different colors, for a black & white shoot.

We went to the top of her building to get a brick background.

I learned that professional photographers never ask you to smile. Excellent.

Photo credit: Beth Kelly. Copyright © 2003.

Once at a book reading, a woman told me I looked much younger than my photo. At a different event, I overheard someone say they must have photo-shopped my photo because I looked so much older in person.

For *The Poe Shadow*, a few years later, we all agreed that I did look different enough that we should do a new photo.

Maybe because I stopped shaving as much.

This time, I was sent with my editor to the studio of Sigrid Estrada, also in New York. Again, wardrobe problems. My poor editor had to iron my sports coat. I thought the wrinkle look was in.

Photo credit: Sigrid Estrada. Copyright © 2006.

At my book readings, I try to keep things light and fun. I'm often told I seem much less serious than my author photos.

At some level, your photos are calibrated to your books. If you're writing a satire, maybe you'd smile more.

I've had the same hair dresser for about nine years now, and he always turns to the author photo and admires his work.

We were all happy with the photo for *The Poe Shadow*, and I voted to use it again for *The Last Dickens* because I pretty much look the same. Ever notice author photos sometimes get frozen and used again and again?

I imagine because, like me, most authors don't like going to the photo studio. I'm now weighing how long I can get away with this one.

Matthew Pearl is the author of The Dante Club, The Poe Shadow, *and* The Last Dickens. *His books have been* New York Times *and international bestsellers, translated into more than thirty languages. He is a graduate of Harvard University and Yale Law School and has taught literature and creative writing at Harvard University and Emerson College and has been a Visiting Lecturer in law and literature at Harvard Law School. He lives in Cambridge, Massachusetts.*

EXERCISE TWO:

Answer the following questions about the blog post, "Surviving the Author Photo."

1. Why does the author include such details as his father's losing the Jimi Hendrix photos and his taking two different-colored shirts to a black-and-white photo shoot?

   _____

   _____

   _____

   _____

   _____

   _____

2. What are some techniques Pearl uses to create and maintain a casual, conversational tone in this piece?

   _____

   _____

   _____

   _____

   _____

3. How relevant are the issues of balance and objectivity in your appreciation of this piece? Why?

   _____

   _____

   _____

   _____

   _____

Writing Opportunity One: Choose a time in your life or an event or experience that you remember fondly but with, perhaps, a sense of comedy, poignancy, etc. Then, write a personal essay in which you attempt to convey to your reader, not only the facts of the event, but also the emotion(s) you associate with it.

Chapter Eight

COMMON LOGICAL FALLACIES AND PROPAGANDA TECHNIQUES

While using this book, you have encountered—and been asked to use—a few words and ideas that might be absolutely new to you. The fact that you can accept or reject someone else's argument, not because you agree or disagree with it, but because you can evaluate the validity of the argument itself is an often-overlooked concept. We somehow tend to labor under the misconception that, since everyone has a right to his or her opinion, all opinions are equal in the consideration we must give them.

This is absolutely not true, as your examination of the opinion-based pieces in the other chapters of this book have probably already shown you. The opinion of a person who has no knowledge or experience to support it is not worth any serious consideration, nor is the argument of a person who has made no attempt to argue fairly and reasonably.

Two key types of arguments that can be rejected as bad arguments are those that employ **logical fallacies** and those that degenerate from argument into **propaganda**. When you learn to recognize the most common fallacies and propaganda techniques, you will be able to improve your own argument as well as your understanding of others' arguments.

Logical Fallacies are exactly what their name suggests—they are errors in logic, faulty reasoning. Usually the person who is basing his or her argument on a logical fallacy is simply mistaken, not aware that the reasoning is flawed. Often, all it takes is to point out the fallacy, and the person will abandon the argument. Likewise, it is important to be able to recognize errors in logic so as not to be drawn into supporting an argument that is, ultimately, flawed.

Depending on your source, there are dozens of logical fallacies. The most common, however, are the self-evident truth, the false or weak analogy, begging the question, the *cum hoc* and *post hoc* fallacies, and the hasty and/or sweeping generalities.

- **The Self-Evident Truth** is quite simply any statement that claims to need no definition or proof. When "it goes without saying..." or "there can be no doubt that..." or "it's patently obvious that...," whoever is making those claims is asserting a self-evident truth. If you happen to agree with the self-evident truth, you may not recognize it as a fallacy. But if you believe the opposite (e.g., there's an undeniable relationship between length of hair and IQ...), then you see how the assertion is not only false, but the arguer has not left any room for disagreement or discussion.

His or her point is so obviously correct, what is there left to discuss?

- **The False or Weak Analogy** is a comparison (an analogy) that is not true (false) or is true in only the most tentative ways. Analogies are powerful tools for helping us clarify our points: each of our employees is like a little cog in the complex machinery of the company—each has its own role, and if any one were to fail, the entire machine would break down.

There's an analogy that, at first glance, sounds pretty good. If we examine the analogy closer, however, we have to wonder how much like a "little cog" a human employee really is. The "cog," probably some kind of gear or pulley or something, does not have a personality. It does not have a "life" beyond its role in the machine. It was probably manufactured on an assembly line along with 10,000 other cogs that are absolutely identical. So, when the one cog fails (breaking down the entire machine), it can be easily replaced and won't really be missed. The machine will be no different with the new cog.

Now how accurate is the comparison of a human employee with a "little cog"?

Of course, *no* analogy is perfect because the two items being compared in an analogy are never identical. When there are too many key points of difference, however, or when the points of similarity are purely superficial or really non-existent, then we have a weak or false analogy.

In the nineteenth century, British philosopher William Paley "proved" the existence of God by comparing the Universe to a watch. A watch, Paley observed, is a complex and intricate mechanism composed of numerous parts, all of which work in a synchronized manner. The Universe, Paley continued, is also complex and intricate and composed of numerous parts that move in a synchronized manner. The watch did not simply happen but was fashioned by a skilled craftsman; the Universe therefore…

Consider the kindergarten teacher who requests not to have the youngest Smith boy put in her class because she had the boy's older brother. The brother had red hair, freckles, and a terrible temper. The youngest Smith boy has red hair, freckles…

The problem with false or weak analogies is that they are very tempting. People like to see correlations. They enjoy defining what they do not know or understand in terms of what they do. This is why analogies are so helpful, and false analogies are so dangerous.

- **Begging the Question** is another common error in logic and can be quite difficult to diagnose. It is also called "Circular Reasoning" and is the fallacy of basing a conclusion on a premise that has not yet been proven or agreed upon.

Suppose at your student council meeting, someone proposes a carwash to raise the money to hire someone to cut down the ugly and overgrown fir tree in front of the school. Two or three students begin to debate when to have the carwash, how to advertise it, or whether a carwash is the best fundraiser to have. The rest of the student council sits silently because *none of you believes the tree needs to be cut down!*

The student who proposed the carwash and the students who began debating it have all begged the question. It must first be established whether or not the tree must come down before you argue about how best to take it down.

Many, many social and political debates fail to find resolution because proponents of *both sides* beg the question and debate Point B before really settling Point A:

- *The unborn have a right to life* (do they?); *therefore, abortion is immoral.*
- *Women have a right to choose* (do they?); *therefore, abortion should be legal.*
- *The United States was founded upon Christian principles* (was it?); *therefore, all laws should be consistent with Christian doctrine.*
- *The United States was founded upon pluralistic and egalitarian principles* (was it?); *therefore, no religion should predominate our legal and judicial systems.*

The simple statement, *If A, then B*, is probably the first bit of logic a person learns. It is a true enough statement. But if we don't carefully establish A to be true and simply jump to conclusion B, we've begged the question and embarked on an invalid argument.

- **The *Cum Hoc, Post Hoc* fallacies** attempt to show a close relationship—usually a cause-and-effect relationship—where there is none. In the *cum hoc* fallacy, two events are observed as occurring at the same time, and one is therefore seen as causing the other. In the autumn, we notice that leaves on trees change color and then fall to the ground. At the same time, we notice that the days grow shorter and colder. Clearly, the falling of the leaves causes a change in the weather (coincidentally, when the leaves grow back in the spring, the days grow warm and light again!).

  The *post hoc* fallacy is similar, but remember that the Latin word *post* means "after." The *post hoc* fallacy, therefore, argues that because one event happened *after* another event, it must have happened *because of* that earlier event. A struggling student notices that the day after he got a haircut he failed a math test, and he vows never to have his hair cut again (at least not on the day before a major test).

- **Hasty Generalities and/or Sweeping Generalities** are very similar to each other and are quite simply careless ways of analyzing and interpreting information. Generalities can be very useful in communicating information quickly and succinctly. Marketers don't need all the raw statistics; they need only be told that the 18- to 25-year-old group tends to download more music than buy CDs. It's more important for a state representative to know that her elderly constituents tend to favor state-supported public transportation than to have a complete statistical breakdown of gender, race, etc. Poorly formed and inaccurate generalizations, however, are at best misleading and potentially even dangerous. As the name suggests, the hasty generality has been arrived at too quickly, before enough data has been gathered and analyzed.

  Film industry analysts love to predict a new movie's overall success by how well it does at the box office the first weekend after it opens. While a hugely successful first weekend might actually entice people to see a movie they otherwise would not have (see the propaganda technique called "Bandwagon"), there have been many cases in which a movie broke box office records its first weekend and then showed poorly in the rest of its run. There have, likewise, been many films that attracted very little attention during the opening weekend but then went on the establish themselves as very popular movies over the long run. To generalize about a film's overall success based on its first weekend attendance is, essentially, a **hasty generality**.

Hasty generalities occur when writers, eager to meet a deadline, speak with too few people or consider only what the first few witnesses had to say.

They occur whenever a person arrives at a general conclusion based on too little evidence:

- *That restaurant is never open; I went there three times, and it was closed.*

- *Mr. J____s never gives extensions on homework assignments; I needed an extra week on my research paper, and he said no.*

- *That newspaper is so biased! Did you read last week's editorial about the mayor?*

The **sweeping generality** is similar to the hasty generality. It might be based on data, but it is too far reaching and does not account for variations in the data.

- A teenaged driver is cut off on the highway by an elderly driver and concludes that citizens over a certain age should have their licenses taken away.

- An elderly driver is cut off on the highway by a teenager and concludes that the minimum driving age needs to be raised.

EXERCISE ONE:

In the spaces provided, note whether each of the following statements is a legitimate statement or a logical fallacy. If it is a logical fallacy, identify it.

1. As the Anatech, Inc., scandal shows, Corporate America cannot be trusted to police its own ranks.

   _____

   _____

   _____

2. The moral and intellectual bankruptcy of the majority party is reason enough to vote every incumbent out of office.

   _____

   _____

   _____

3. Most dentists in the nationwide survey advised their patients not to chew gum at all.

   _____

   _____

   _____

4. You can't deny that all forms of mass media are biased.

   _____

   _____

   _____

5. One can't help but notice that the excessive spring rains and flooding in the Midwest started just as Halley's Comet appeared in astronomers' telescopes.

   _____

   _____

   _____

6. With the cost of prescription medicines too high for many Americans without health insurance, it is imperative for Congress to act quickly on this legislation.

_____

_____

_____

7. The United States has created a modern-day Roman Empire in the Middle East.

_____

_____

_____

8. Last week's loss indicates a serious inadequacy in Coach Brunden's coaching style.

_____

_____

_____

9. Authorities say that no cause has been identified, but it must be noted that the accident occurred only moments after an owl was trapped in the barn of Sarah McFarsdale on Blenham Street.

_____

_____

_____

10. Thirty-six hours of torrential rains and tides several feet higher than normal severely weakened the earthen levees so that, on Sunday, April 22, at 3:07 p.m., they broke and sank the city under several feet of water.

_____

_____

_____

Propaganda is the intentional manipulation of information or language in order to essentially trick or mislead an inattentive or naïve audience into accepting the conclusion of the propagandist. While the work of the propagandist is sometimes obvious in its tone and effect, most propaganda is subtle and seductive to even educated and thoughtful persons. It's interesting to note that, sometimes, the only difference between a logical fallacy and propaganda is intent. Propaganda is an *intentional* departure from reason and legitimate argument.

Assertion (unsupported claim) is arguably the most innocently employed technique of propaganda, but it is also the easiest one to guard against. All writers make assertions; a writer's thesis is his or her assertion. Nearly every example, fact, or statistic used to support the thesis is introduced by an assertion. The assertion becomes propaganda only when it is left to stand alone, without argument, discussion, and support. The problem with the logical fallacy *begging the question* is that the conclusion is based on an unsupported and unproved assertion. The *self-evident truth* is also a form of unsupported assertion. Whether the writer intentionally offers no support (perhaps because there is none or what there is is unconvincing), or whether he or she honestly believes that no support is necessary, the careful reader must demand some examples, definition, statistics, or whatever before accepting the writer's thesis as valid.

- Razor-tongued vice-presidential candidate Spiro Agnew dismissed student protesters against the United States' military involvement by saying that they had "never done a productive thing in their lives" and "They take their tactics from Fidel Castro and their money from daddy" (quotations from several public addresses during the 1968 presidential election).

- While campaigning for the Republican nomination for president in 2007, Senator John McCain combined the techniques of the **unsupported claim** and appeals to fear and consequences when he told his South Carolina audience, "If we leave Iraq there will be chaos, there will be genocide, and they will follow us home" (Associated Press, 26 April 2007). Military experts in the Bush administration responded that this claim was, indeed, unfounded.

- In a guest sermon delivered on Father's Day, 2008, then-presidential candidate Barack Obama admonished his audience, "If we are honest with ourselves, we'll admit that what too many fathers also are is missing...They have abandoned their responsibilities ... You and I know how true this is in the African-American community" (Huffington Post 15 June 2008). Later, syndicated columnist Kenneth Brooks criticized what he considered to be Mr. Obama's **unsupported assertions**: "Obama provides no factual support for his claim that characteristics in African-American culture are responsible for African-American males abandoning their parental duties and for causing other problems in the African-American community. Lacking this factual support, his conclusions are worthless" ("*Ethicalego* Opinion," 21 July 2008).

Name-Calling is perhaps the most common propaganda technique and possibly the easiest to recognize. It is the propagandist's way of dehumanizing his or her target. Just about every nationality and ethnic group has one or more derogatory term for persons of other nationalities and ethnic groups. It is easier to hate—and to perform injustices and cruelties to—these nonhuman Others. Enemies in wartime will also often practice name-calling to fuel the war's enmity.

Most propagandistic name-calling, however, is more subtle. To call an opponent a "pig" or a "viper" may seem harmless, but the propagandist hopes his or her audience will attach some of the negative associations to the person being called the name. Vipers are venomous, and they hide in wait for their prey. Thus, the politician called a "viper" in an editorial is attacked as dishonest and dangerous. Pigs are stereotypically lazy, stupid, and dirty, and the propagandist intends the person called a "pig" to seem that way in the reader's mind.

Often credited with the creation of the politics of personal defamation, then-Vice President Spiro Agnew derided protesters of United States' military involvement in Vietnam saying, "A spirit of national masochism prevails, encouraged by an effete corps of **impudent snobs who characterize themselves as intellectuals**" (quotations from a speech delivered 19 October 1969).

"Snob," "yuppie," "bum," "redneck," "Yankee" are all names that are used to dehumanize the Other, making it easier for the propagandist to denounce them and for the propagandist's followers to treat them badly, even criminally.

Card-stacking (stacking the deck) actually has its roots in legitimate argument. Highlighting facts that are most pertinent to the audience and that support the writer's thesis is at the very definition of slant and spin. To blatantly *ignore* facts to the contrary, however, especially if the opposing facts outnumber (or outweigh in quality) the facts presented, indicates that the writer is not arguing fairly; he or she has become a propagandist.

Exaggeration can be a legitimate language device. If used excessively, however, or in conjunction with other techniques like appeal to emotions or name-calling, it can entice readers to cast aside reason and arrive at an inappropriately strong conclusion.

- To note the presence of a cockroach in a restaurant kitchen might raise a legitimate concern, but a single roach would not warrant a description of *roach-infested*.

- A tired and hungry teenager may unadvisedly respond rudely to the police officer who has pulled him over for a speeding ticket, but one surly comment does not necessarily show the teenager to be *hostile*.

Appeals to…

…Emotion (emotion-laden words) are rooted in simple good writing. When used excessively, however, their use becomes propaganda. Beginning with elementary school, writers are taught to use vivid and powerful words—*frigid* instead of *very cold*, *devastating* instead of *very bad*, and so on. Many of these powerful words do not carry extremely emotional connotations (*red*, versus *scarlet*, versus *crimson*; *wet*, versus *saturated*, versus *soaked*), but many of these words evoke strong emotional responses in readers, and they can be used precisely for their emotional appeal. *Deplorable* is more than a description; it is a judgment. *Pitiable, slaughter, heroic,* and *sacrifice* are all emotional words that can be used by the propagandist to carry the reader to an inference considerably beyond where the facts might lead.

- To call a parentless child an *orphan* is a fact. To refer to the child, who was driven from her home when an invading army destroyed her village, a *refugee* is a fact. To refer to either child's *pathetic smile* as he or she receives a Red Cross care package is to appeal to readers' emotions rather than their reason.

…Fear are specific appeals to emotion, usually treated separately because they are so powerful. The propagandist who appeals to his or her readers' fears is intentionally attempting to initiate the readers' "fight or flight" response, when reason shuts off and the readers' only concern is to protect themselves and their loved ones.

- When then-Vice President Spiro Agnew asserted, "Confronted with the choice, the American people would choose the policeman's truncheon over the **anarchist's bomb**," he was employing several techniques of the propagandist, but he was first and foremost preying on the middle-American's fear that the then-current changes occurring in United States society were all negative, and the country would soon plunge into complete lawlessness.

- In August 2009, former vice-presidential candidate Sarah Palin criticized a proposed national healthcare bill by writing, "The America I know and love is not one in which my parents or my baby with Down Syndrome will have to stand in front of Obama's '**death panel**'…," clearly preying on the fears of elderly and chronically ill Americans.

- During the 1964 presidential election, President Lyndon Johnson's campaign ran a television ad now famously referred to as "Daisy Girl" or "Peace, Little Girl." The advertisement showed a little girl in a meadow, plucking the petals off of a daisy. Eventually, a menacing voice replaced hers, counting down from 10, until at 0, the audience sees a missile streak across the sky, and the screen goes black. The voice of Johnson then says, "These are the stakes! To make a world in which all of God's children can live, or to go into the dark. We must either love each other, or we must die." Another announcer then says, "Vote for President Johnson on November 3. The **stakes are too high** for you to stay home." This advertisement, which was played only once on national television, was a strong appeal to audiences' fear of the possibility of a nuclear war.

- In the 2008 race for the Democratic presidential nomination, candidate Senator Hillary Clinton's campaign ran a television advertisement not unlike 1964's "Daisy Girl." Clinton's ad showed a little child asleep in bed while an announcer said, "It's 3 a.m. and your children are safe and asleep. But there's a phone in the White House, and it's ringing. … Your vote will decide who answers that call, whether it's someone … ready to lead in a **dangerous** world." The final line is a clear appeal to voters' fear instead of their reason.

...**Flattery (apple-polishing)** actually can work two ways. First, of course, the propagandist sidesteps the validity (or invalidity) of the argument and instead compliments and cajoles the reader into accepting the thesis:

- *Intelligent and educated readers will immediately see the advantages of my proposal...*
- *No thinking person can disagree that...*

Second, the propagandist insults the opposition, thus tacitly implying that the reader agrees with the argument:

- *Only a fool would continue to think that...*
- *Of course, there are those with less training and experience who might want to argue that...*

Either way, the propagandist is no longer arguing rationally, no longer focusing on facts, analysis, or interpretation. He or she is no longer even providing opinion and support but simply trying to trick the reader into agreement.

...**Consequences (*argumentum ad consequentiam*)** combine elements of appeal to emotions (especially fear) and appeal to flattery. The technique suggests a cause-and-effect relationship between the point in the argument and some— usually exaggerated—outcome. If the outcome is negative, the propagandist is appealing to the reader's fear. If it is positive, he or she is appealing to flattery. In either case, the cause-effect relationship is either untrue (see the *cum hoc* and *post hoc* fallacies) or hugely exaggerated. The technique works—as do most techniques of propaganda—by distracting the reader from the real issue, the argument.

- *If this bill is allowed to pass, insurance companies will soon have the authority to make life and death decisions on your behalf.*
- *If this bill is allowed to pass, health insurance will be available and affordable to every citizen of the United States.*
- *People will continue to die if a traffic light is not installed at this intersection.*
- *Imagine the nightmarish tie-ups that will be the result of a traffic light at this intersection.*

Pinpointing the Enemy (scapegoating) is similar to name-calling, but perhaps a bit more overt with a stronger intention. As name-calling dehumanizes the Other and seduces the reader into accepting injustice or cruelty toward that Other, pinpointing the enemy actually identifies that Other as the cause of the propagandist's (and the readers') problems. Having identified the enemy, the reader is then justified in hating—even seeking to destroy—that enemy. The problem, of course, is that in most instances, pinpointing a single enemy is a gross oversimplification of the issue. Still, it is easier for the propagandist to entice the reader to hate a single person or group than to examine the full complexities of the issue and try to devise a rational solution.

- Probably the most graphic example of **pinpointing the enemy** in recent history is the Holocaust. As Germany faced severe economic problems in the wake of the First World War, the Nazi regime succeeded in convincing the German people that the Jews—a large number of whom were bankers and lawyers—were at the root of all of Germany's problems. Eliminate the Jews, the Nazis insisted, and Germany's problems would be over.

- Both Republicans and Democrats in the United States like to identify **scapegoats** on whom to blame the problems facing the nation. Depending on the crisis and the party, recently **pinpointed enemies** have included "big government," illegal aliens, Wall Street brokers and investors, Wal-Mart, insurance companies, AM radio, and the American consumer.

Oversimplification and Stereotyping are closely related to pinpointing the enemy. Most issues are more complex than "either A or B." As we discussed when we first introduced **spin** in Chapter Three, there are usually at least two sides to every story. Still, readers often prefer to have their information presented to them "in a nutshell" rather than having to sift through pages and pages of raw, unanalyzed, and uninterpreted data. The result is, however, if the reader never examines the data, he or she runs the risk of assuming that the "nutshell" is all there is to an issue.

- *"To some extent I would say this; if you've seen one city slum, you've seen them all."* —*Spiro Agnew, Governor of Maryland, 1968.*

- *If people hadn't tried to buy houses they couldn't really afford, we wouldn't have a foreclosure crisis right now.*

241

- *Studies of voter turnout in recent elections clearly illustrate the extent of voter apathy in this nation.*

- *If kids didn't spend all their time playing video games, we wouldn't have problems with adolescent obesity, diabetes, and illiteracy.*

False Dilemma (lesser of two evils) is another common technique of the propagandist, and it draws heavily on oversimplification, appeals to fear and flattery, and begging the question. Just as oversimplification takes a multifaceted issue and reduces it to a "nutshell," the **false dilemma** reduces a complex, multifaceted issue to a simple (or oversimplified) *either . . . or*. Problems in argument arise when the two horns of the dilemma (1) are not the only two sides of the story or (2) are not really mutually exclusive.

- A famous political cartoon, attributed to Benjamin Franklin, circulated the thirteen American colonies in the early eighteenth century to illustrate the need for the thirteen separate colonies to unite and form a confederation for their collective dealings with Great Britain. The cartoon depicts a snake severed into pieces, each labeled with the initials of a colony or area. The caption reads, "Join or die." Clearly, joining the First Continental Congress or ceasing to exist as a colony were not the *only* two options available, but the cartoon was effective in convincing colonists to support the Congress and its decisions.

- Writer and activist Eldridge Cleaver, as the presidential candidate for the "Peace and Freedom Party," asserted to voters that they were "either part of the solution or part of the problem." The false dilemma here, of course, preys on people's desire not to be part of the problem. It is implied, however, that one must side with the speaker in order to be a part of the solution. There is a middle ground in which a thoughtful person can disagree with the speaker's proposed solution and still help devise a solution rather than be a perpetuator of the problem.

Similar to the false dilemma is the **lesser of two evils** technique. Here, the propagandist not only reduces the issue to two alternatives, but he or she convinces the reader that both alternatives are undesirable, only one is less so.

- *You can get a flu vaccination and risk actually getting the flu, or you can skip the shot and risk getting an even worse case later on.*

- *You can finance your purchase now and pay exorbitant finance charges, or you can save the money, only to see the price of the item increase.*

As with the false dilemma, the two alternatives presented in the lesser of two evils are rarely the *only two* options available, and at least one of them is usually not as bad as the propagandist would have it seem.

EXERCISE TWO:

In the spaces provided, note whether each of the following statements is a legitimate statement or an example of propaganda. If it is propaganda, identify the technique. Because some of the techniques are so similar to others or involve the use of other techniques, you may note more than one for some of the statements you identify as propaganda. It is much more important that you recognize the propagandist at work than that you be able to name the technique he or she is using.

1. Do you *really* want your children to attend school with a [*insert the gender, age, racial, ethnic, national, religious, etc., epithet of your choice*]?

   _____

   _____

   _____

2. Reports from state departments of health to the Centers for Disease Control and Prevention in Atlanta indicate a strong correlation between vaccinations and a decrease in incidence of disease.

   _____

   _____

   _____

3. The choice is clear: more funding for school or increased unemployment and crime.

   _____

   _____

   _____

4. When the last glacier melts and Denver, Colorado, is a seaside resort, we'll all wish we'd voted for this Clean Energy Bill.

   _____

   _____

   _____

5. We call all Americans to thank their Creator for the precious blessings of liberty and abundance.

_____

_____

_____

6. For good, honest, reliable labor, hire a real American.

_____

_____

_____

7. Either we place stringent restrictions on the insurance industry, or we continue to provide inadequate healthcare to a large percentage of our citizens.

_____

_____

_____

8. Would they have us believe that "justice" includes allowing murderers and pedophiles to walk freely among us?

_____

_____

_____

9. Apathetic and lazy teenagers make no contribution whatsoever to this city.

_____

_____

_____

10. Support term limits and put an end to corruption in government!

_____

_____

_____

11. Although single parents comprise almost 50% of the city's population, there is only one single parent on the seven-member city council.

_____

_____

_____

12. When Senator Newley makes these claims, we have to wonder whether he's a liar or simply insane.

_____

_____

_____

13. The wretched sight of mere children growing up in squalor would move even the coldest-hearted among us to action.

_____

_____

_____

14. Mortgage foreclosures were down 8% from last quarter; new applications for unemployment benefits were down 3%; home sales were up .5%; consumer shopping was up 1%.

_____

_____

_____

15. At the current rates of production and consumption, industry analysts estimate that the world honey supply will be completely depleted in 71 years, 5 months, 6 days, and 14 hours.

_____

_____

_____

16. This Election Day, say no to high taxes and low services; vote Joe for mayor!

_____

_____

_____

17. Unnecessary medical procedures and medications do more harm than good.

_____

_____

_____

18. How can we let children in famine-struck nations starve when the United States produces so much surplus milk and grain that we can just give them?

_____

_____

_____

19. The sheer idiocy of this administration's course of action can lead only to utter disaster.

_____

_____

_____

20. We can ration gasoline today, or we can all walk tomorrow.

_____

_____

_____

21. When that inevitable tragedy strikes, don't you want to be prepared?

_____

_____

_____

22. Private schools are too expensive, and public schools are simply unsafe; there is only one way to properly educate our children.

_____

_____

_____

23. If you've lost your job or home this year, write a letter to the governor and thank her for bankrupting your state.

_____

_____

_____

24. While we may resist any change in our comfortable lifestyles, do we really want to risk the alternative?

_____

_____

_____

25. No rational person can believe Dockingham's claims to have witnessed that historic event.

_____

_____

_____

26. We must wrest our government from the hands of the thick-headed bigots who are currently in control.

_____

_____

_____

27. All loyal voters will undoubtedly recognize the legitimacy of this claim.

_____

_____

_____

28. The benefits of this policy are innumerable, and those who support it will earn the undying devotion of their constituents.

_____

_____

_____

29. Glaciers in Greenland are retreating faster than originally estimated; the Antarctic ice cap is shrinking at an alarming rate; Western Europe has experienced three consecutive summers of deadly, record-setting high temperatures...

_____

_____

_____

30. The assassins who operate those clinics should be executed for capital murder.

_____

_____

_____

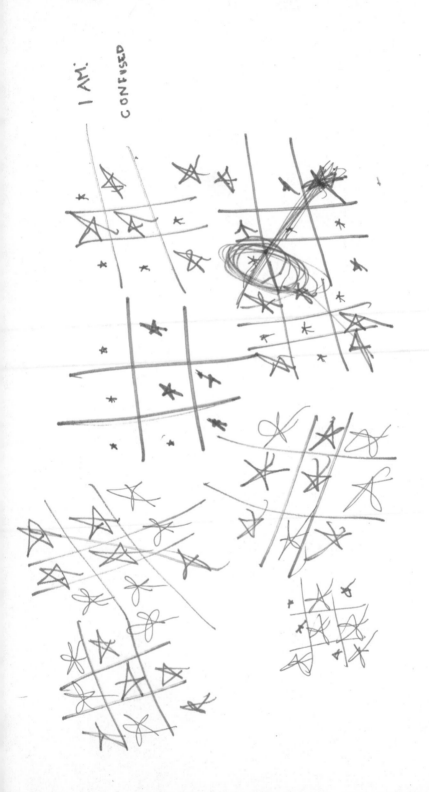